Mediterranean Diet Air Fryer Cookbook

Easy and Delicious Mediterranean Recipes with Complete Guide to Master Your Air Fryer on A Budget

Judy Flanke

Content

Part I

Introduction

Air-Frying for Mediterranean Dieters: Healthy Frying for Weight Loss and Improved Well-being

Food has always been a passion of mine. I have always enjoyed the flavor that is created when certain ingredients are combined and the various renditions of classic recipes that I can quickly whip up in my kitchen. The only challenge I experienced when it came to food was not realizing which foods were contributing to my well-being and which were not. I would stuff whatever tasted good down my throat without considering the healthier alternatives or exceptions to the dish. I knew that it was an unsustainable lifestyle and that my eating habits had to change. My wake-up call came when I saw a loved one survive breast cancer. Her doctor had recommended that she follow a post-treatment diet to reduce the risks of any further disease forming in her body. The recommended diet was none other than the Mediterranean diet. This diet has been shown in many studies to reduce the risk of cancers, heart disease, diabetes, and levels of bad cholesterol.

Motivated by the improvements I witnessed in her life, I was also determined to switch to the Mediterranean diet. Unlike other diets, I knew that this one wouldn't force me to eliminate any foods out of my diet or restrict the number of calories I consumed. It did however challenge me to reflect on my food choices and base my diet on mostly healthy foods which provided nutritional benefits. The Mediterranean diet food pyramid simply emphasized the importance of incorporating leafy vegetables, fruits, legumes, whole grains, and lean protein in my diet while consuming decadent foods like ice-cream or a glass of wine on very few occasions. I quickly realized that the Mediterranean diet was more of a lifestyle than a militant diet and this encouraged me to create new eating habits.

In this cookbook, I desire to share with you some of the most delicious Mediterranean diet recipes I have gathered over the years that are extremely popular with my friends and family. However, there is a twist. The recipes that I present to you are all made using one of the most highly talked-about kitchen gadgets—an air fryer. I will explain the ways in which you can create healthy Mediterranean-inspired meals using your air fryer without compromising on the nutritional value of your dishes. Get ready to learn how to make innovative meals that promote a balanced well-being!

Chapter 1: Frying Mediterranean Delicacies

The Mediterranean Lifestyle

When you think of the Mediterranean diet, does your mind gravitate toward Italian pizzas and French bread? While these popular European dishes are tasty, they are not exactly good examples of what we mean when we speak of the Mediterranean diet. The diet originates from the traditional eating practices that were common in regions along the Mediterranean sea. In years gone by, people living in this region relied on a diet that was based on traditional vegetables, fruits, beans, nuts, seafood, plenty of olive oil, and dairy—served with a glass of wine of course. This is how the people living in Crete, Greece, and Southern Italy ate around the 1960s when their rates of chronic disease were recorded as being one of the lowest and their life expectancy recorded as being one of the highest in the world.

A traditional Mediterranean diet is largely based on fruits, olive oil, seafood, nuts, and vegetables which leads to a significantly reduced risk of mental and physical illness. Some of the health problems that you can avoid by following a Mediterranean diet include heart disease, stroke, Parkinson's disease, obesity, and type 2 diabetes. Even though the benefits of this diet have been studied and proven by many doctors and researchers, there are still many misconceptions circulating about how the diet works. The first myth is that it is expensive to switch to the Mediterranean diet. This is not true. In fact, it is more affordable to adopt a Mediterranean diet because most meals are prepared from plant-based foods, fruits, nuts, and other whole-foods that can easily be sourced from food markets at a fraction of the cost of processed or packaged foods.

The second myth is that a diet of pasta and bread constitutes a Mediterranean diet. Generally, Mediterraneans don't eat as much pasta as Americans do. In meals, pasta is usually a side dish served in a serving size of between half a cup and a full cup. The rest of their plate usually consists of vegetables, salads, a portion of fish, and maybe a slice or two of bread. The third and probably the most disappointing myth is that the Mediterranean diet is only about food. Even though food forms a large part of the diet, there are other aspects of the Mediterranean diet that promote a healthy and balanced lifestyle. For example, Mediterraneans strongly encourage sitting down on a table to enjoy a relaxing meal. Food is shared across the table, allowing everyone's plate to include various food groups that promote a balanced meal. Mediterraneans also enjoy physical activity and will typically take a walk after meals to allow the food to settle in their stomachs.

5 Tips for Switching to the Mediterranean Lifestyle

If you're considering making a lifestyle change and embracing the Mediterranean diet, you don't have to feel overwhelmed by the new eating habits that you will need to adopt. For the most part, your diet will remain the same with the exception of cutting down on bad fats, decadent foods, and processed meals. Below are some tips to help you make the switch to the Mediterranean diet:

1.Eat Lots of Vegetables

Vegetables can be prepared in a number of ways and surprisingly, are also very filling! They will provide you with all of the minerals and vitamins you need to maintain good health, improve your skin, detoxify your body, improve your emotional moods, and maintain energy throughout the day. Vegetables can be chopped up in a salad, blended in a soup, or served as a side dish in every meal.

2.Always Eat Breakfast

Breakfast is the first opportunity you get to wake your body up and break the fasting from the night before. Eating healthy breakfasts consisting of fruit, whole grains, and other high-fiber foods will give you the energy required to sustain you throughout the day and keep you fuller for longer.

3.Cook a Vegetarian Meal Once Per Week

Ever heard of "Meatless Mondays?" This craze has been trending around the world to promote a lifestyle that is not meat-dependent. While meat is allowed on a Mediterranean diet, the saturated fats found in meat products make it less favorable to consume frequently. Try going a day without eating meat and instead, create your meals using beans, whole grains, and vegetables. Once you get the hang of it, try going two days a week without consuming any meat.

4. Consume Dairy Products in Moderation

The United States Department of Agriculture (USDA) recommends that saturated fats (typically found in meat and dairy products) make up no more than 10% of your daily calorie intake. For most people, this means limiting saturated fats to 200 calories per day. This will allow you to enjoy dairy products such as cheese and yogurt in moderation.

5. Enjoy Fruits As Dessert Options

Once again, desserts are allowed on a Mediterranean diet. However, the higher the sugar content of the dessert, the more unhealthy the dessert becomes. Sometimes a bowl of ice cream is appropriate but other times you can opt for a more healthier option like fresh strawberry sorbet, frozen grapes, or apples dipped in honey.

Nonetheless, the true Mediterranean diet is more than adopting a plant-based diet. It is also about incorporating daily physical exercise like walking or swimming and sharing meals with others. The act of engaging in a meaningful discussion around the dinner table can improve your overall mood and reduce stress. Eating with others also prevents overeating, as meals are shared and dialogue is enjoyed in between every mouthful. Mediterraneans create a social atmosphere around eating and use it as a time for connecting with loved ones or expanding one's social network. At the end of the day, connecting with people over food will regulate your eating habits, deepen the relationships you have with others, as well as improve your emotional, mental, and physical well-being.

Mediterranean Cooking with the Air Fryer

If you thought that by switching to the Mediterranean way of living you would have to give up fried foods, think again! With the popular invention of the air fryer, you are able to create healthy Mediterranean-inspired recipes that are not drenched in oil or cause adverse health risks. The truth is that the process of deep-frying food adds a lot of fat to food than when other methods of cooking are used. For example, a 100-gram oven-roasted chicken breast contains around 0.39 grams of fat while a battered and deep-fried alternative contains 13.2 grams of fat. Even with this information, many people would still opt to eat the deep-fried chicken breast over the oven-roasted one due to the unmatched flavor and texture that it offers.

An air fryer removes the guilt from consuming fried-food because the process of achieving that same crispy texture we love is completely different. This allows health-conscious folk to enjoy fried-foods that contain lower fat content than food cooked in a deep fryer. Air fryers work by simply circulating around food to the same crispiness as deep-fried foods. The major difference between air frying and deep-frying is that with the former, you only need a fraction of the oil while achieving a similar flavor and texture. In other words, the air fryer removes high-fat and high-calorie oils from the process of making fried foods. All it takes is a teaspoon of cooking oil (instead of several cups) to create crispy chicken, sweet potatoes, or kale chips.

When used in the proper manner, air fryers can provide you with many health benefits. Firstly, it can promote weight loss. Those who love to consume deep-fried foods will consume fewer calories when preparing their fried food recipes using an air fryer. Secondly, air fryers are a lot safer to use than regular deep fryers. The process of deep frying food involves heating a saucepan or pot full of scalding oil. Many times, when the oil gets too hot, it can spill or splatter across your stovetop and cause burns on your skin. Although air fryers do become hot, there is no risk of being burned with oil when using them. Nevertheless, it is always recommended to follow the air fryer manual for safe and convenient cooking.

Furthermore, when frying foods using the traditional deep frying method, you can expose yourself to dangerous compounds such as acrylamide, that form in certain foods during deep frying. Acrylamide, for instance, has been known to have links to some cancers including ovarian, breast, endometrial, and pancreatic cancer. By simply switching to an air fryer, you will reduce your exposure to acrylamide and other lethal compounds formed in the process of high-heat cooking.

The Secret to Preparing Healthy Air-Fried Foods

I fell in love with the air fryer due to the hands-off style cooking that it offers. I didn't have to wrestle with hot oil anymore and hope that it doesn't splatter on my clothes or hands. One thing that I quickly learned about frying foods with an air fryer is that to achieve the best results, I had to put in a lot more thought than simply turning it on and walking away. Below are a few tips and suggestions for cooking high-quality crispy food and achieving the desired flavor and texture using your air fryer:

1.How to Achieve Even Cooking in an Air Fryer

The best way to achieve an even crispy coating on your foods is to avoid overfilling your air fryer. The circulation of hot air can be compromised when there is too much food packed tightly together, and causing the food to steam instead of frying evenly. When arranging your food in the air fryer, organize it in a puzzle formation, placing smaller pieces in the gaps between bigger pieces. When cooking protein, flip the meat or fish around half-way through cooking so that both sides receive an equal amount of heat. Avoid using your hands when flipping your meats as this may cause serious burns. Instead, use a pair of kitchen tongs for a quick and controlled grip

2.How to Achieve Better Browning in an Air Fryer

To brown your meat and vegetables using an air fryer, simply pat the meat or vegetables down with a tea towel to remove excess moisture from the surface. Doing this will also prevent your food from steaming as it cooks through, providing you with a more crispy result. Cooking with fat can also help to brown your food in an air fryer. While many will try to avoid using fat, adding just a little bit to your food will produce tasty results! If you are really not a fan of fat, you can substitute it with a little bit of honey. The sugar in the honey will aid in browning your meat or vegetables, as well as adding a great flavor. If you are cooking pastry dough in the air fryer, brush the dough with egg yolk before placing it in the fryer to give it a glossy brown coating when it has cooked through.

3.How to Achieve a Crunchier Coating Using an Air Fryer

One of the best tips that you can keep in your back pocket and use when air frying crispy chicken or vegetables, is to first pre-toast your bread or corn crumbs before coating your food with it. To pre-toast your bread or corn crumbs, drizzle a little oil on them and pop them in the microwave for a few minutes. They should come out looking golden-brown and simply irresistible!

4.How to Cook Juicy Steaks in an Air Fryer

The first tip when cooking steaks in your air fryer is to cut them down in size so that you are able to fit more meat in your basket. After cutting your large steak pieces, add a seasoning or spice rub on each piece so that your meat is generously coated. Try to use seasonings that are darker in color and stronger in flavor to give your steak a better overall color and taste the cooking is complete.

5.How to Cook Fish in an Air Fryer

The first tip when cooking fish in an air fryer is to cook it on a lower heat setting. While steaks can handle a blast of heat from an air fryer, your fish will come out looking and tasting a lot better on a lower heat. Fish will also require a longer time to cook through so that it is prepared in the most non-aggressive way. Cooking your fish on a low temperature for longer will also give it time to develop a crispy crust and the golden-brown color that we all love! You can also skewer your fish to allow for an easier removal out of the air fryer once it has been cooked. When air frying extremely delicate fish, place a sheet of foil on the base of the basket so that your fish does not stick to the bottom or break after cooking.

6.How to Cook Tender Chicken in an Air Fryer

The number one tip for cooking chicken in an air fryer is to place your chicken pieces skin side up. This is because the heat in an air fryer comes from above. When turning your chicken pieces over, ensure that on the final turn the skin is facing up to give it the time to crisp in direct heat. For even crispier and flavorful pieces of chicken, poke your meat with a skewer or fork to make a few holes in between the skin, allowing some of the chicken's oily juices to come out and brown the chicken even more.

7.How to Make Complete Meals Using an Air Fryer

Did you know that you can use an air fryer to prepare dinner from start to finish? There are a few tips on how to successfully do this. Firstly, learn how to stack your dinner in the air fryer. You can layer all of your dinner ingredients one on top of the other. For instance, placing vegetables directly under protein will allow the two to cook simultaneously and allow the oil juices from the meat to baste the vegetables below. Moreover, use the microwave to prepare sauces or a simple side as your food cooks in the air fryer. The microwave can also be used to partially cook certain foods before being placed in the air fryer, thereby shortening the overall cook time.

The Air Fryer Cooking Chart

Once you have an idea of the kinds of air frying recipes you desire to try out, it is important to learn about the various cooking times for each food. The cooking chart below will show you a comprehensive list of cooking times and temperature settings to use when making some of your favorite dishes. All fryers, depending on their models, will differ slightly in how they are designed so take this cooking chart as a general guideline. It is the perfect starting point to manage your time wisely when placing various foods in your air fryer.

Vegetables					
INGREDIENT	AMOUNT	PREPARATION	OIL	TEMP	COOK TIME
Asparagus	2 bunches	Cut in half, trim stems	2 Tbsp	420°F	12-15 mins
Beets	1½ lbs	Peel, cut in ½-inch cubes	1Tbsp	390°F	28-30 mins
Bell peppers (for roasting)	4 peppers	Cut in quarters, remove seeds	1Tbsp	400°F	15-20 mins
Broccoli	1 large head	Cut in 1-2-inch florets	1Tbsp	400°F	15-20 mins
Brussels sprouts	1lb	Cut in half, remove stems	1Tbsp	425°F	15-20 mins
Carrots	1lb	Peel, cut in ¼-inch rounds	1 Tbsp	425°F	10-15 mins
Cauliflower	1 head	Cut in 1-2-inch florets	2 Tbsp	400°F	20-22 mins
Corn on the cob	7 ears	Whole ears, remove husks	1 Tbps	400°F	14-17 mins
Green beans	1 bag (12 oz)	Trim	1 Tbps	420°F	18-20 mins
Kale (for chips)	4 oz	Tear into pieces, remove stems	None	325°F	5-8 mins
Mushrooms	16 oz	Rinse, slice thinly	1 Tbps	390°F	25-30 mins
Potatoes, russet	1½ lbs	Cut in 1-inch wedges	1 Tbps	390°F	25-30 mins
Potatoes, russet	1lb	Hand-cut fries, soak 30 mins in cold water, then pat dry	½ -3 Tbps	400°F	25-28 mins
Potatoes, sweet	1lb	Hand-cut fries, soak 30 mins in cold water, then pat dry	1 Tbps	400°F	25-28 mins
Zucchini	1lb	Cut in eighths lengthwise, then cut in half	1 Tbps	400°F	15-20 mins

Beef

Item	Temp (°F)	Time (mins)	Item	Temp (°F)	Time (mins)
Beef Eye Round Roast (4 lbs.)	400 °F	45 to 55	Meatballs (1-inch)	370 °F	7
Burger Patty (4 oz.)	370 °F	16 to 20	Meatballs (3-inch)	380 °F	10
Filet Mignon (8 oz.)	400 °F	18	Ribeye, bone-in (1-inch, 8 oz)	400 °F	10 to 15
Flank Steak (1.5 lbs.)	400 °F	12	Sirloin steaks (1-inch, 12 oz)	400 °F	9 to 14
Flank Steak (2 lbs.)	400 °F	20 to 28			

Chicken

Item	Temp (°F)	Time (mins)	Item	Temp (°F)	Time (mins)
Breasts, bone in (1 ¼ lb.)	370 °F	25	Legs, bone-in (1 ¾ lb.)	380 °F	30
Breasts, boneless (4 oz)	380 °F	12	Thighs, boneless (1 ½ lb.)	380 °F	18 to 20
Drumsticks (2 ½ lb.)	370 °F	20	Wings (2 lb.)	400 °F	12
Game Hen (halved 2 lb.)	390 °F	20	Whole Chicken	360 °F	75
Thighs, bone-in (2 lb.)	380 °F	22	Tenders	360 °F	8 to 10

Pork & Lamb

Item	Temp (°F)	Time (mins)	Item	Temp (°F)	Time (mins)
Bacon (regular)	400 °F	5 to 7	Pork Tenderloin	370 °F	15
Bacon (thick cut)	400 °F	6 to 10	Sausages	380 °F	15
Pork Loin (2 lb.)	360 °F	55	Lamb Loin Chops (1-inch thick)	400 °F	8 to 12
Pork Chops, bone in (1-inch, 6.5 oz)	400 °F	12	Rack of Lamb (1.5 – 2 lb.)	380 °F	22

Fish & Seafood

Item	Temp (°F)	Time (mins)	Item	Temp (°F)	Time (mins)
Calamari (8 oz)	400 °F	4	Tuna Steak	400 °F	7 to 10
Fish Fillet (1-inch, 8 oz)	400 °F	10	Scallops	400 °F	5 to 7
Salmon, fillet (6 oz)	380 °F	12	Shrimp	400 °F	5
Swordfish steak	400 °F	10			

Part II
About the Recipes

The selection of recipes below was carefully considered to introduce you to the Mediterranean diet through air-fried foods. You will experience flavors that are common and some that will take you on a journey to the Mediterranean sea. Get ready to be blown away by the skillful use of healthy ingredients that will satisfy your savory and sweet cravings while offering you a lot of nutritional value too! Are you trying to go down a dress size? These delicious recipes will allow you to lose weight, improve your overall well-being, and boost your body's natural energy without having to restrict any foods. At the end of the day, it's all about consuming foods in moderation, and enjoying life in between!

CHAPTER 2

BREAKFAST

Mushroom and Spinach Cups

- Olive oil cooking spray
- 6 large eggs
- 1 garlic clove, minced
- ½ teaspoon salt
- ½ teaspoon black pepper
- Pinch red pepper flakes
- 8 ounces (227 g) baby bella mushrooms, sliced
- 1 cup fresh baby spinach
- 2 scallions, white parts and green parts, diced

1. Preheat the air fryer to 320ºF (160ºC). Lightly coat the inside of six silicone muffin cups or a six-cup muffin tin with olive oil cooking spray.
2. In a large bowl, beat the eggs, garlic, salt, pepper, and red pepper flakes for 1 to 2 minutes, or until well combined.
3. Fold in the mushrooms, spinach, and scallions.
4. Divide the mixture evenly among the muffin cups.
5. Place into the air fryer and bake for 12 to 15 minutes, or until the eggs are set.
6. Remove and allow to cool for 5 minutes before serving.

Spinach and Mushroom Frittata

- Olive oil cooking spray
- 8 large eggs
- ½ teaspoon salt
- ½ teaspoon black pepper
- 1 garlic clove, minced
- 2 cups fresh baby spinach
- 4 ounces (113 g) baby bella mushrooms, sliced
- 1 shallot, diced
- ½ cup shredded Swiss cheese, divided
- Hot sauce, for serving (optional)

1. Preheat the air fryer to 360ºF (182ºC). Lightly coat the inside of a 6-inch round cake pan with olive oil cooking spray.
2. In a large bowl, beat the eggs, salt, pepper, and garlic for 1 to 2 minutes, or until well combined.
3. Fold in the spinach, mushrooms, shallot, and ¼ cup of the Swiss cheese.
4. Pour the egg mixture into the prepared cake pan, and sprinkle the remaining ¼ cup of Swiss over the top.
5. Place into the air fryer and bake for 18 to 20 minutes, or until the eggs are set in the center.
6. Remove from the air fryer and allow to cool for 5 minutes. Drizzle with hot sauce (if using) before serving.

Parmesan Egg Pita

Prep time: 5 minutes | Cook time: 6 minutes | Serves 2

- 1 whole wheat pita
- 2 teaspoons olive oil
- ½ shallot, diced
- ¼ teaspoon garlic, minced
- 1 large egg

- ¼ teaspoon dried oregano
- ¼ teaspoon dried thyme
- ⅛ teaspoon salt
- 2 tablespoons shredded Parmesan cheese

1. Preheat the air fryer to 380ºF (193ºC).
2. Brush the top of the pita with olive oil, then spread the diced shallot and minced garlic over the pita.
3. Crack the egg into a small bowl or ramekin, and season it with oregano, thyme, and salt.
4. Place the pita into the air fryer basket, and gently pour the egg onto the top of the pita. Sprinkle with cheese over the top.
5. Bake for 6 minutes.
6. Allow to cool for 5 minutes before cutting into pieces for serving.

Cinnamon Muffins with Pecans

Prep time: 15 minutes | Cook time: 13 minutes | Makes 12 muffins

- 4 cups whole wheat flour
- 1 tablespoon ground cinnamon
- 2 teaspoons baking soda
- 2 teaspoons allspice
- 1 teaspoon ground cloves
- 1 teaspoon salt

- 1 cup cashew butter
- 2 cups honey
- 2 large eggs, lightly beaten
- 2 cups unsweetened applesauce
- ¼ cup chopped pecans
- 1 to 2 tablespoons oil

1. In a large bowl, whisk the flour, cinnamon, baking soda, allspice, cloves, and salt until blended.
2. In another large bowl, combine the butter and honey. Using an electric mixer, beat the mixture for 2 to 3 minutes until light and fluffy. Add the beaten eggs and stir until blended.
3. Add the flour mixture and applesauce, alternating between the two and blending after each addition. Stir in the pecans.
4. Preheat the air fryer to 325ºF (163ºC). Spritz 12 silicone muffin cups with oil.
5. Pour the batter into the prepared muffin cups, filling each halfway. Place the muffins on the air fryer tray.
6. Air fry for 6 minutes. Shake the basket and air fry for 7 minutes more. The muffins are done when a toothpick inserted into the middle comes out clean.

Vanilla-Blueberry Pancake Poppers

Prep time: 5 minutes | Cook time: 8 minutes | Makes 8 pancake poppers

- 1 cup whole wheat flour
- 1 tablespoon honey
- 1 teaspoon baking soda
- ½ teaspoon baking powder
- 1 cup unsweetened almond milk
- 1 large egg
- 1 teaspoon vanilla extract
- 1 teaspoon olive oil
- ½ cup fresh blueberries

1. In a medium mixing bowl, combine the flour, honey, baking soda, and baking powder and mix well.
2. Mix in the milk, egg, vanilla, and oil.
3. Coat the inside of an air fryer muffin tin with cooking spray.
4. Fill each muffin cup two-thirds full. (You may have to bake the poppers in more than one batch.)
5. Drop a few blueberries into each muffin cup.
6. Set the muffin tin into the air fryer basket.
7. Set the temperature to 320ºF (160ºC). Set the timer and bake for 8 minutes.
8. Insert a toothpick into the center of a pancake popper; if it comes out clean, they are done. If batter clings to the toothpick, cook the poppers for 2 minutes more and check again.
9. When the poppers are cooked through, use silicone oven mitts to remove the muffin tin from the air fryer basket. Turn out the poppers onto a wire rack to cool.

Rosemary Potato Fries with Garlic

Prep time: 5 minutes | Cook time: 16 minutes | Serves 4

- 2 cups cubed potato (small cubes from 2 medium potatoes)
- 1½ teaspoons olive oil
- 3 medium cloves garlic, minced or pressed
- ¼ teaspoon sea salt
- ¼ teaspoon onion granules
- ⅛ teaspoon freshly ground black pepper
- Cooking oil spray
- ½ tablespoon dried rosemary or fresh rosemary, minced

1. In a medium bowl, toss the potatoes with the oil, garlic, salt, onion granules, and black pepper. Stir to evenly coat the potatoes with the seasonings. Place the potato mixture in the air fryer basket and roast at 390ºF (199ºC) for 8 minutes. Set the bowl aside.
2. Remove, shake the basket or stir the contents and cook for another 8 minutes, or until the potatoes are tender and nicely browned. Add the potatoes back to the bowl and spray with oil. Add the rosemary, toss, and serve immediately.

Whole Wheat Biscuits

Prep time: 10 minutes | Cook time: 9 to 10 minutes | Serves 5

- 4 cups whole wheat flour
- 1 tablespoon baking powder
- 1 teaspoon salt
- 6 tablespoons cashew butter, plus

- more for brushing on the biscuits (optional)
- ¾ cup unsweetened coconut milk
- 1 to 2 tablespoons oil

1. In a large bowl, whisk the flour, baking powder, and salt until blended.
2. Add the cashew butter. Using a pastry cutter or 2 forks, work the dough until pea-size balls of the butter-flour mixture appear. Stir in the coconut milk until the mixture is sticky.
3. Preheat the air fryer to 330ºF (166ºC). Line the air fryer tray with parchment paper and spritz it with oil.
4. Drop the dough by the tablespoonful onto the prepared tray, leaving 1 inch between each, to form 10 biscuits.
5. Bake for 5 minutes. Flip the biscuits and cook for 4 minutes more for a light brown top, or 5 minutes more for a darker biscuit. Brush the tops with the butter, if desired.

Paprika Hash Browns

Prep time: 5 minutes | Cook time: 20 minutes | Serves 4

- 4 russet potatoes
- 1 teaspoon paprika
- Salt

- Pepper
- Cooking oil

1. Peel the potatoes using a vegetable peeler. Using a cheese grater, shred the potatoes. If your grater has different-size holes, use the area of the tool with the largest holes.
2. Place the shredded potatoes in a large bowl of cold water. Let sit for 5 minutes. Cold water helps remove excess starch from the potatoes. Stir to help dissolve the starch.
3. Drain the potatoes and dry with paper towels or napkins. Make sure the potatoes are completely dry.
4. Season the potatoes with the paprika and salt and pepper to taste.
5. Spray the potatoes with cooking oil and transfer them to the air fryer. Cook at 370ºF (188ºC) for 20 minutes, shaking the basket every 5 minutes (a total of 4 times).
6. Cool before serving.

Apples Stuffed with Granola

- 4 Granny Smith or other firm apples
- 1 cup granola
- 2 tablespoons coconut sugar
- ¾ teaspoon cinnamon
- 2 tablespoons cashew butter
- 1 cup water or apple juice

1. Working one apple at a time, cut a circle around the apple stem and scoop out the core, taking care not to cut all the way through to the bottom. (This should leave an empty cavity in the middle of the apple for the granola.) Repeat with the remaining apples.
2. In a small bowl, combine the granola, coconut sugar, and cinnamon. Pour the butter over the ingredients and stir with a fork. Divide the granola mixture among the apples, packing it tightly into the empty cavity.
3. Place the apples in the cake pan insert for the air fryer. Pour the water or juice around the apples. Bake at 350ºF (177ºC) for 20 minutes until the apples are soft all the way through.
4. Serve warm with a dollop of crème fraîche or yogurt, if desired.

Zucchini and Refried Bean Tacos

- Cooking oil spray
- 1 small zucchini
- 1 small-medium yellow onion
- ¼ teaspoon garlic granules
- ⅛ teaspoon sea salt
- Freshly ground black pepper
- 1 (15-ounce / 425-g) can vegan refried beans
- 6 corn tortillas
- Fresh salsa of your choice
- 1 avocado, cut into slices, or fresh guacamole

1. Spray the air fryer basket with the oil. Cut the zucchini and onion and place in the air fryer basket. Spray with more oil and sprinkle evenly with the garlic, salt, and pepper to taste. Roast at 390ºF (199ºC) for 6 minutes. Remove, shake or stir well, and cook for another 6 minutes, or until the veggies are nicely browned and tender.
2. In a small pan, warm the refried beans over low heat. Stir often. Once to temperature, remove from the heat and set aside.
3. To prepare the tortillas, sprinkle them individually with a little water, then place in a hot skillet (in a single layer; you may need to do this in batches), turning over as each side becomes hot.
4. To make the breakfast tacos: Place a corn tortilla on your plate and fill it with beans, roasted vegetables, salsa, and avocado slices.

Sweet Potato Hash with Mushrooms

Prep time: 15 minutes | Cook time: 18 minutes | Serves 6

- 2 medium sweet potatoes, peeled and cut into 1-inch cubes
- ½ green bell pepper, diced
- ½ red onion, diced
- 4 ounces (113 g) baby bella mushrooms, diced
- 2 tablespoons olive oil
- 1 garlic clove, minced
- ½ teaspoon salt
- ½ teaspoon black pepper
- ½ tablespoon chopped fresh rosemary

1. Preheat the air fryer to 380ºF (193ºC).
2. In a large bowl, toss all ingredients together until the vegetables are well coated and seasonings distributed.
3. Pour the vegetables into the air fryer basket, making sure they are in a single even layer. (If using a smaller air fryer, you may need to do this in two batches.)
4. Cook for 9 minutes, then toss or flip the vegetables. Cook for 9 minutes more.
5. Transfer to a serving bowl or individual plates and enjoy.

Honey Blueberry Muffins

Prep time: 10 minutes | Cook time: 15 minutes | Serves 6

- Olive oil cooking spray
- ½ cup unsweetened applesauce
- ¼ cup honey
- ½ cup plain Greek yogurt
- 1 teaspoon vanilla extract
- 1 large egg
- 1½ cups plus 1 tablespoon whole wheat flour, divided
- ½ teaspoon baking soda
- ½ teaspoon baking powder
- ½ teaspoon salt
- ½ cup blueberries, fresh or frozen

1. Preheat the air fryer to 360ºF (182ºC). Lightly coat the inside of six silicone muffin cups or a six-cup muffin tin with olive oil cooking spray.
2. In a large bowl, combine the applesauce, honey, yogurt, vanilla, and egg and mix until smooth.
3. Sift in 1½ cups of the flour, the baking soda, baking powder, and salt into the wet mixture, then stir until just combined.
4. In a small bowl, toss the blueberries with the remaining 1 tablespoon flour, then fold the mixture into the muffin batter.
5. Divide the mixture evenly among the prepared muffin cups and place into the basket of the air fryer. Bake for 12 to 15 minutes, or until golden brown on top and a toothpick inserted into the middle of one of the muffins comes out clean.
6. Allow to cool for 5 minutes before serving.

Peach Oatmeal

Prep time: 5 minutes | Cook time: 30 minutes | Serves 6

- Olive oil cooking spray
- 2 cups certified gluten-free rolled oats
- 2 cups unsweetened almond milk
- ¼ cup honey, plus more for drizzling (optional)
- ½ cup plain Greek yogurt
- 1 teaspoon vanilla extract
- ½ teaspoon ground cinnamon
- ¼ teaspoon salt
- 1½ cups diced peaches, divided, plus more for serving (optional)

1. Preheat the air fryer to 380ºF (193ºC). Lightly coat the inside of a 6-inch cake pan with olive oil cooking spray.
2. In a large bowl, mix together the oats, almond milk, honey, yogurt, vanilla, cinnamon, and salt until well combined.
3. Fold in ¾ cup of the peaches and then pour the mixture into the prepared cake pan.
4. Sprinkle the remaining peaches across the top of the oatmeal mixture. Bake in the air fryer for 30 minutes.
5. Allow to set and cool for 5 minutes before serving with additional fresh fruit and honey for drizzling, if desired.

Red Potatoes with Red Bell Pepper

Prep time: 10 minutes | Cook time: 20 to 22minutes | Serves 4

- 2 cups diced waxy red potatoes
- 2 teaspoons olive oil, divided
- Kosher salt, to taste
- ½ cup chopped yellow onion
- 1 cup chopped red bell pepper
- 1¾ cups ketchup
- 2 chipotle peppers in adobo plus 1 tablespoon adobo sauce
- ½ teaspoon smoked paprika

1. In a medium bowl, toss the potatoes with 1 teaspoon of oil and season with a pinch of salt. Place them in the air fryer basket and cook at 400ºF (204ºC) for 10 minutes. In the meantime, in a small bowl toss the onion and pepper with the remaining teaspoon of oil and season with salt.
2. After 10 minutes, add the onion and pepper to the air fryer basket and toss to combine. Cook for an additional 10 to 12 minutes until the peppers are softened and charred at the edges and the potatoes are crispy outside and cooked through.
3. While the vegetables are cooking, prepare the chipotle ketchup. Combine the ketchup, 2 chipotle peppers, and 1 tablespoon of the adobo sauce in a blender and purée until smooth. Pour the chipotle ketchup into a serving bowl.
4. When the vegetables are cooked, remove them from the air fryer and toss them with the smoked paprika. Serve immediately with chipotle ketchup on the side.

CHAPTER 3

APPETIZERS

Shrimp with Garlic Olive Oil

Prep time: 15 minutes | Cook time: 6 minutes | Serves 4

- 1 pound (454 g) medium shrimp, cleaned and deveined
- ¼ cup plus 2 tablespoons olive oil, divided
- Juice of ½ lemon
- 3 garlic cloves, minced and divided
- ½ teaspoon salt
- ¼ teaspoon red pepper flakes
- Lemon wedges, for serving (optional)
- Marinara sauce, for dipping (optional)

1. Preheat the air fryer to 380ºF (193ºC).
2. In a large bowl, combine the shrimp with 2 tablespoons of the olive oil, as well as the lemon juice, ⅓ of the minced garlic, salt, and red pepper flakes. Toss to coat the shrimp well.
3. In a small ramekin, combine the remaining ¼ cup of olive oil and the remaining minced garlic.
4. Tear off a 12-by-12-inch sheet of aluminum foil. Pour the shrimp into the center of the foil, then fold the sides up and crimp the edges so that it forms an aluminum foil bowl that is open on top. Place this packet into the air fryer basket.
5. Roast the shrimp for 4 minutes, then open the air fryer and place the ramekin with oil and garlic in the basket beside the shrimp packet. Cook for 2 more minutes.
6. Transfer the shrimp on a serving plate or platter with the ramekin of garlic olive oil on the side for dipping. You may also serve with lemon wedges and marinara sauce, if desired.

Cheddar Portobello Mushrooms

Prep time: 10 minutes | Cook time: 10 minutes | Serves 5

- 8 ounces (227 g) large portobello mushrooms
- ⅓ cup salsa
- ½ cup shredded Cheddar cheese
- Cooking oil

1. Cut the stem out of the mushrooms: First, chop off the end of the stem, and then make a circular cut around the area where the stem was. Continue to cut until you have removed the rest of the stem.
2. Stuff the mushrooms with the salsa. Sprinkle the shredded cheese on top.
3. Place the mushrooms in the air fryer. Cook at 370ºF (188ºC) for 8 minutes.
4. Cool before serving.

Basil Cherry Tomatoes and Olives

Prep time: 5 minutes | Cook time: 20 minutes | Serves 6

- 2 cups cherry tomatoes
- 4 garlic cloves, roughly chopped
- ½ red onion, roughly chopped
- 1 cup black olives
- 1 cup green olives
- 1 tablespoon fresh basil, minced
- 1 tablespoon fresh oregano, minced
- 2 tablespoons olive oil
- ¼ to ½ teaspoon salt

1. Preheat the air fryer to 380°F (193°C).
2. In a large bowl, combine all of the ingredients and toss together so that the tomatoes and olives are coated well with the olive oil and herbs.
3. Pour the mixture into the air fryer basket, and roast for 10 minutes. Stir the mixture well, then continue roasting for an additional 10 minutes.
4. Remove from the air fryer, transfer to a serving bowl, and enjoy.

Buffalo Cauliflower Bites

Prep time: 10 minutes | Cook time: 25 minutes | Serves 4

- 1 cup whole wheat flour
- 1 cup water
- 1 teaspoon garlic powder
- 1 large head cauliflower, cut into florets
- Cooking oil
- ⅓ cup Frank's RedHot Buffalo Wings sauce

1. In a large bowl, combine the flour, water, and garlic powder. Mix well. The mixture should resemble pancake batter.
2. Add the cauliflower to the batter and stir to coat. Transfer the cauliflower to another large bowl to drain the excess batter.
3. Spray the air fryer with cooking oil.
4. Transfer the cauliflower to the air fryer. Do not stack. Cook in batches. Spray the cauliflower with cooking oil. Cook at 370°F (188°C) for 6 minutes.
5. Open the air fryer and transfer the cauliflower to a large bowl. Drizzle with the Buffalo sauce. Mix well.
6. Return the cauliflower to the air fryer. Cook for an additional 6 minutes, or until crisp.
7. Remove the cooked cauliflower from the air fryer, then repeat steps 4 through 6 for the remaining cauliflower batches.
8. Cool before serving.

Red Pepper Tapenade with Olives

Prep time: 5 minutes | Cook time: 5 minutes | Serves 4

- 1 large red bell pepper
- 2 tablespoons plus 1 teaspoon olive oil, divided
- ½ cup Kalamata olives, pitted and
- roughly chopped
- 1 garlic clove, minced
- ½ teaspoon dried oregano
- 1 tablespoon lemon juice

1. Preheat the air fryer to 380ºF (193ºC).
2. Brush the outside of a whole red pepper with 1 teaspoon olive oil and place it inside the air fryer basket. Roast for 5 minutes.
3. Meanwhile, in a medium bowl combine the remaining 2 tablespoons of olive oil with the olives, garlic, oregano, and lemon juice.
4. Remove the red pepper from the air fryer, then gently slice off the stem and remove the seeds. Roughly chop the roasted pepper into small pieces.
5. Add the red pepper to the olive mixture and stir all together until combined.
6. Serve with pita chips, crackers, or crusty bread.

Chicken Wings with Honey Mustard

Prep time: 10 minutes | Cook time: 24 minutes | Serves 2

- 2 pounds (907 g) chicken wings
- Salt and freshly ground black pepper
- 2 tablespoons cashew butter
- ¼ cup honey
- ¼ cup spicy brown mustard
- Pinch ground cayenne pepper
- 2 teaspoons Worcestershire sauce

1. Prepare the chicken wings by cutting off the wing tips and discarding (or freezing for chicken stock). Divide the drumettes from the wingettes by cutting through the joint. Place the chicken wing pieces in a large bowl.
2. Preheat the air fryer to 400ºF (204ºC).
3. Season the wings with salt and freshly ground black pepper and air fry the wings in two batches for 10 minutes per batch, shaking the basket half way through the cooking process.
4. While the wings are air frying, combine the remaining ingredients in a small saucepan over low heat.
5. When both batches are done, toss all the wings with the honey-mustard sauce and toss them all back into the basket for another 4 minutes to heat through and finish cooking. Give the basket a good shake part way through the cooking process to redistribute the wings. Remove the wings from the air fryer and serve.

Artichoke Pita Flatbread with Olives

Prep time: 5 minutes | Cook time: 10 minutes | Serves 4

- 2 whole wheat pitas
- 2 tablespoons olive oil, divided
- 2 garlic cloves, minced
- ¼ teaspoon salt
- ½ cup canned artichoke hearts,
- sliced
- ¼ cup Kalamata olives
- ¼ cup shredded Parmesan
- ¼ cup crumbled feta
- Chopped fresh parsley, for garnish (optional)

1. Preheat the air fryer to 380ºF (193ºC).
2. Brush each pita with 1 tablespoon olive oil, then sprinkle the minced garlic and salt over the top.
3. Distribute the artichoke hearts, olives, and cheeses evenly between the two pitas, and place both into the air fryer to bake for 10 minutes.
4. Remove the pitas and cut them into 4 pieces each before serving. Sprinkle parsley over the top, if desired.

Cream Cheese and Crab Wontons

Prep time: 10 minutes | Cook time: 8 minutes | Serves 5

- 4 ounces (113 g) ⅓-less-fat cream cheese, at room temperature
- ½ cup lump crab meat, picked over for bits of shell
- 2 scallions, chopped
- 2 garlic cloves, finely minced
- 2 teaspoons reduced-sodium soy sauce
- 15 wonton wrappers
- 1 large egg white, beaten
- 5 tablespoons Thai sweet chili sauce, for dipping

1. In a medium bowl, combine the cream cheese, crab, scallions, garlic, and soy sauce. Mix with a fork until thoroughly combined.
2. Working with one at a time, place a wonton wrapper on a clean surface, the points facing top and bottom like a diamond. Spoon 1 level tablespoon of the crab mixture onto the center of the wrapper. Dip your finger in a small bowl of water and run it along the edges of the wrapper. Take one corner of the wrapper and fold it up to the opposite corner, forming a triangle. Gently press out any air between wrapper and filling and seal the edges. Set aside and repeat with the remaining wrappers and filling. Brush both sides of the wontons with egg white.
3. Preheat the air fryer to 340ºF (171ºC).
4. Working in batches, arrange a single layer of the wontons in the air fryer basket. Cook for about 8 minutes, flipping halfway, until golden brown and crispy. Serve hot with the chili sauce for dipping.

Air Fried Okra

Prep time: 15 minutes | Cook time: 10 minutes | Serves 4

- 1½ cups okra, cut into ¼-inch pieces
- 3 tablespoons unsweetened coconut milk
- 2 tablespoons whole wheat flour
- 2 tablespoons cornmeal
- Salt
- Pepper
- Cooking oil

1. Make sure the okra pieces are dry, using paper towels if needed.
2. Pour the coconut milk into a small bowl. In another small bowl, combine the flour and cornmeal, and season with salt and pepper to taste.
3. Spray the air fryer basket with cooking oil.
4. Dip the okra in the coconut milk, then the flour and cornmeal.
5. Place the okra in the air fryer basket. It is okay to stack it. Spray the okra with cooking oil. Cook at 380ºF (193ºC) for 5 minutes.
6. Open the air fryer and shake the basket. Cook for an additional 5 minutes, or until the okra is crisp.
7. Cool before serving.

Breaded Green Tomatoes

Prep time: 15 minutes | Cook time: 30 minutes | Serves 4

- 2 green tomatoes
- 2 eggs
- ½ cup whole wheat flour
- ½ cup yellow cornmeal
- ½ cup whole wheat bread crumbs
- 1 teaspoon garlic powder
- Salt
- Pepper
- Cooking oil

1. Cut the tomatoes into ½-inch-thick rounds.
2. In a small bowl, beat the eggs. In another small bowl, place the flour. In a third small bowl, combine the yellow cornmeal and bread crumbs, and season with the garlic powder and salt and pepper to taste. Mix well to combine.
3. Spray the air fryer basket with cooking oil.
4. Dip each tomato slice in the flour, then the egg, and then the cornmeal and bread crumb mixture.
5. Place the tomato slices in the air fryer. Do not stack. Cook in batches. Spray the tomato slices with cooking oil. Cook at 400ºF (204ºC) for 5 minutes.
6. Open the air fryer and flip the tomatoes. Cook for an additional 4 to 5 minutes, or until crisp.
7. Remove the cooked tomato slices from the air fryer, then repeat steps 5 and 6 for the remaining tomatoes.

Tomatillo and Jalapeño Salsa Verde

Prep time: 10 minutes | Cook time: 24 minutes | Serves 4

- 1 large poblano pepper
- 1 large jalapeño
- ¼ small onion
- 2 garlic cloves
- Olive oil spray
- ¾ pound (340 g) tomatillos, husks removed
- 3 tablespoons chopped fresh cilantro
- 1 teaspoon kosher salt

1. Preheat the air fryer to 400ºF (204ºC).
2. Spritz the poblano, jalapeño, onion, and garlic with olive oil, then transfer to the air fryer basket. Cook for about 14 minutes, flipping halfway, until charred on top. (For a toaster oven–style air fryer, the temperature remains the same; cook for 10 minutes.) Remove the poblano, wrap in foil, and let it cool for 10 minutes. Remove the remaining vegetables from the basket and transfer to a food processor.
3. Spritz the tomatillos with oil and place in the air fryer basket. Cook for 10 minutes, flipping halfway, until charred. Transfer to the food processor with the other vegetables.
4. Unwrap the foil from the poblano. Peel the skin off and remove the seeds. Transfer to the food processor along with the cilantro, and salt. Pulse the mixture until the ingredients are coarsely chopped. Add 5 to 6 tablespoons water and pulse until a coarse puree forms. Transfer the salsa to a serving dish.

Dill Pickle Chips

Prep time: 10 minutes | Cook time: 10 minutes | Serves 4

- 1 pound (454 g) whole dill pickles
- 2 eggs
- $1/_3$ cup whole wheat flour
- $1/_3$ cup whole wheat bread crumbs
- Cooking oil

1. Cut the pickles crosswise into ½-inch-thick slices. Dry the slices completely using a paper towel.
2. In a small bowl, beat the eggs. In another small bowl, add the flour. Place the bread crumbs in a third small bowl.
3. Spray the air fryer basket with cooking oil.
4. Dip the pickle slices in the flour, then the egg, and then the bread crumbs.
5. Place the breaded pickle slices in the air fryer. It is okay to stack them. Spray them with cooking oil. Cook at 400ºF (204ºC) for 6 minutes.
6. Open the air fryer and flip the pickles. Cook for an additional 2 to 3 minutes, or until the pickles are crisp.

Basil Crostini with Goat Cheese

Prep time: 5 minutes | Cook time: 5 minutes | Serves 4

- 1 whole wheat baguette
- ¼ cup olive oil
- 2 garlic cloves, minced
- 4 ounces (113 g) goat cheese
- 2 tablespoons fresh basil, minced

1. Preheat the air fryer to 380ºF (193ºC).
2. Cut the baguette into ½-inch-thick slices.
3. In a small bowl, mix together the olive oil and garlic, then brush it over one side of each slice of bread.
4. Place the olive-oil-coated bread in a single layer in the air fryer basket and bake for 5 minutes.
5. Meanwhile, in a small bowl, mix together the goat cheese and basil.
6. Remove the toast from the air fryer, then spread a thin layer of the goat cheese mixture over the top of each piece and serve.

Crab Cakes with Red Bell Pepper

Prep time: 10 minutes | Cook time: 10 minutes | Serves 6

- 8 ounces (227 g) lump crab meat
- 2 tablespoons diced red bell pepper
- 1 scallion, white parts and green parts, diced
- 1 garlic clove, minced
- 1 tablespoon capers, minced
- 1 tablespoon plain Greek yogurt
- 1 egg, beaten
- ¼ cup whole wheat bread crumbs
- ¼ teaspoon salt
- 1 tablespoon olive oil
- 1 lemon, cut into wedges

1. Preheat the air fryer to 360ºF (182ºC).
2. In a medium bowl, mix the crab, bell pepper, scallion, garlic, and capers until combined.
3. Add the yogurt and egg. Stir until incorporated. Mix in the bread crumbs and salt.
4. Divide this mixture into 6 equal portions and pat out into patties. Place the crab cakes into the air fryer basket in a single layer, making sure that they don't touch each other. Brush the tops of each patty with a bit of olive oil.
5. Bake for 10 minutes.
6. Remove the crab cakes from the air fryer and serve with lemon wedges on the side.

Crispy Kale Chips

Prep time: 5 minutes | Cook time: 10 minutes | Serves 4

- 1 bunch fresh kale, ribs removed, chopped into large pieces
- 1 tablespoon extra-virgin olive oil
- Salt
- Pepper

1. In a large bowl, combine the kale and olive oil, and season with salt and pepper. Mix well to ensure the kale is fully coated.
2. Place the kale in the air fryer basket. Cook at 275°F (135°C) for 5 minutes.
3. Open the air fryer and shake the basket. Cook for an additional 5 minutes.
4. Cool before serving.

Parmesan Clam Dip with Celery

Prep time: 15 minutes | Cook time: 18 minutes | Serves 6

- Cooking spray
- 2 (6½-ounce / 184-g) cans chopped clams, in clam juice
- ⅓ cup whole wheat bread crumbs
- 1 medium garlic clove, minced
- 1 tablespoon olive oil
- 1 tablespoon fresh lemon juice
- ¼ teaspoon Tabasco sauce
- ½ teaspoon onion powder
- ¼ teaspoon dried oregano
- ¼ teaspoon freshly ground black pepper
- ⅛ teaspoon kosher salt
- ½ teaspoon sweet paprika
- 2½ tablespoons freshly grated Parmesan cheese
- 2 celery stalks, cut into 2-inch pieces

1. Spray a 5½- to 6½-inch round baking dish with cooking spray.
2. Drain one of the cans of clams. Place in a medium bowl along with the remaining can of clams (including the juice), the bread crumbs, garlic, olive oil, lemon juice, Tabasco sauce, onion powder, oregano, pepper, salt, ¼ teaspoon of the paprika, and 2 tablespoons of the Parmesan. Mix well and let sit for 10 minutes. Transfer to the baking dish.
3. Preheat the air fryer to 325°F (163°C).
4. Place the baking dish in the air fryer basket and cook for 10 minutes. Top with the remaining ¼ teaspoon paprika and ½ tablespoon Parmesan. Cook for about 8 more minutes, until golden brown on top. Serve hot, with the celery for dipping.

Cheddar Jalapeño Balls

Prep time: 15 minutes | Cook time: 15 minutes | Makes 12 cheese balls

- 4 ounces (113 g) cream cheese
- ⅓ cup shredded mozzarella cheese
- ⅓ cup shredded Cheddar cheese
- 2 jalapeños, finely chopped
- ½ cup whole wheat bread crumbs
- 2 eggs
- ½ cup whole wheat flour
- Salt
- Pepper
- Cooking oil

1. In a medium bowl, combine the cream cheese, mozzarella, Cheddar, and jalapeños. Mix well.
2. Form the cheese mixture into balls about an inch thick. Using a small ice cream scoop works well.
3. Arrange the cheese balls on a sheet pan and place in the freezer for 15 minutes. This will help the cheese balls maintain their shape while frying.
4. Spray the air fryer basket with cooking oil.
5. Place the bread crumbs in a small bowl. In another small bowl, beat the eggs. In a third small bowl, combine the flour with salt and pepper to taste, and mix well.
6. Remove the cheese balls from the freezer. Dip the cheese balls in the flour, then the eggs, and then the bread crumbs.
7. Place the cheese balls in the air fryer. (It is okay to stack them.) Spray with cooking oil. Cook at 400ºF (204ºC) for 8 minutes.
8. Open the air fryer and flip the cheese balls. I recommend flipping them instead of shaking so the balls maintain their form. Cook an additional 4 minutes.
9. Cool before serving.

Amaretto-Glazed Shrimp with Almonds

Prep time: 20 minutes | Cook time: 40 to 50 minutes | Serves 10 to 12

- 1 cup whole wheat flour
- ½ teaspoon baking powder
- 1 teaspoon salt
- 2 eggs, beaten
- ½ cup unsweetened almond milk
- 2 tablespoons olive oil

- 2 cups sliced almonds
- 2 pounds (907 g) large shrimp (about 32 to 40 shrimp), peeled and deveined, tails left on
- 2 cups amaretto liqueur

1. Combine the flour, baking powder and salt in a large bowl. Add the eggs, milk and oil and stir until it forms a smooth batter. Coarsely crush the sliced almonds into a second shallow dish with your hands.
2. Dry the shrimp well with paper towels. Dip the shrimp into the batter and shake off any excess batter, leaving just enough to lightly coat the shrimp. Transfer the shrimp to the dish with the almonds and coat completely. Place the coated shrimp on a plate or baking sheet and when all the shrimp have been coated, freeze the shrimp for an 1 hour, or as long as a week before air frying.
3. Preheat the air fryer to 400ºF (204ºC).
4. Transfer 8 frozen shrimp at a time to the air fryer basket. Air fry for 6 minutes. Turn the shrimp over and air fry for an additional 4 minutes. Repeat with the remaining shrimp.
5. While the shrimp are cooking, bring the Amaretto to a boil in a small saucepan on the stovetop. Lower the heat and simmer until it has reduced and thickened into a glaze–about 10 minutes.
6. Remove the shrimp from the air fryer and brush both sides with the warm amaretto glaze. Serve warm.

CHAPTER 4

VEGETABLES

Parmesan Hasselback Potatoes

Prep time: 10 minutes | Cook time: 25 minutes | Serves 4 to 5

- 1½ pounds (680 g) baby Yukon Gold potatoes
- 5 tablespoons cashew butter
- Salt and freshly ground black pepper
- 1 tablespoon vegetable oil
- ¼ cup grated Parmesan cheese (optional)
- Chopped fresh parsley or chives

1. Preheat the air fryer to 400ºF (204ºC).
2. Make six to eight deep vertical slits across the top of each potato about three quarters of the way down. Make sure the slits are deep enough to allow the slices to spread apart a little, but don't cut all the way through the potato. Place a thin layer of butter between each of the slices and season generously with salt and pepper.
3. Transfer the potatoes to the air fryer basket. Pack them in next to each other. It's alright if some of the potatoes sit on top or rest on another potato. Air fry for 20 minutes.
4. Spray or brush the potatoes with a little vegetable oil and sprinkle the Parmesan cheese on top (if using). Air fry for an additional 5 minutes. Garnish with chopped parsley or chives and serve hot.

Cardamom-Orange Carrots with Chives

Prep time: 15 minutes | Cook time: 30 minutes | Serves 4

- 2 tablespoons cashew butter
- 1 tablespoon honey
- ½ teaspoon grated orange zest plus 1 tablespoon juice
- ½ teaspoon ground cardamom
- Salt and pepper
- 2 pounds (907 g) carrots, peeled and cut into 2-inch lengths, thick ends halved lengthwise
- 1 tablespoon minced fresh chives

1. Microwave butter, honey, orange zest, cardamom, and ¼ teaspoon salt in large bowl at 50 percent power, stirring occasionally, about 1 minute. Whisk to combine. Combine 1 tablespoon butter mixture and orange juice in small bowl; set aside. Add carrots to remaining butter mixture and toss to coat; transfer to air fryer basket.
2. Place basket in air fryer and set temperature to 400ºF (204ºC). Cook carrots until tender and browned, about 30 minutes, tossing every 10 minutes.
3. Transfer carrots to now-empty bowl and toss with reserved butter mixture. Season with salt and pepper to taste and sprinkle with chives. Serve.

Lemon Potatoes with Rosemary

Prep time: 10 minutes | Cook time: 12 minutes | Serves 4

- 1 pound (454 g) small red-skinned potatoes, halved or cut into bite-sized chunks
- 1 tablespoon olive oil
- 1 teaspoon finely chopped fresh rosemary
- ¼ teaspoon salt
- Freshly ground black pepper
- 1 tablespoon lemon zest

1. Preheat the air fryer to 400ºF (204ºC).
2. Toss the potatoes with the olive oil, rosemary, salt and freshly ground black pepper.
3. Air fry for 12 minutes (depending on the size of the chunks), tossing the potatoes a few times throughout the cooking process.
4. As soon as the potatoes are tender to a knifepoint, toss them with the lemon zest and more salt if desired.

Cheese Zucchini Rice Fritters

Prep time: 15 minutes | Cook time: 10 to 12 minutes | Serves 4

- 3 cups (495 g) cooked rice
- 2 cups grated cheese, such as Cheddar, Swiss, or Gruyère
- 1 medium zucchini, grated
- 4 scallions, white and light green parts only, sliced
- ¼ cup tightly packed chopped fresh mint
- 3 eggs, beaten
- Kosher salt and pepper to taste
- 1¼ cups whole wheat bread crumbs
- Vegetable oil for spraying
- Lemon wedges for serving

1. Combine the cooked rice, grated cheese, grated zucchini, scallions, and mint in a large bowl. Add the beaten eggs and season with salt and pepper. Stir to combine, making sure the egg is evenly distributed through the rice.
2. Spread the bread crumbs on a plate. Scoop out approximately ½ cup (82.5 g) of the rice mixture and form into a ball with your hands, pressing firmly to make the fritters as tight and well-packed as possible. Dredge the ball in the bread crumbs. Repeat with the remaining rice mixture. You should be able to make 8 or 9 fritters. Place half the fritters on a plate and chill until needed.
3. Spray the remaining half of the rice fritters and the basket of the air fryer with oil to prevent sticking. Place the fritters in the basket of the air fryer and cook at 400ºF (204ºC) until browned on all sides and cooked through, 10 to 12 minutes. Carefully remove the fritters to a platter and place the remaining fritters in the air fryer and cook in the same manner. Serve the rice fritters with lemon wedges for spritzing.

Sugar Snap Peas and Carrots with Sesame

Prep time: 10 minutes | Cook time: 16 minutes | Serves 4

- 1 pound (454 g) carrots, peeled sliced on the bias (½-inch slices)
- 1 teaspoon olive oil
- Salt and freshly ground black pepper
- ⅓ cup honey
- 1 tablespoon sesame oil
- 1 tablespoon soy sauce
- ½ teaspoon minced fresh ginger
- 4 ounces (113 g) sugar snap peas
- 1½ teaspoons sesame seeds

1. Preheat the air fryer to 360ºF (182ºC).
2. Toss the carrots with the olive oil, season with salt and pepper and air fry for 10 minutes, shaking the basket once or twice during the cooking process.
3. Combine the honey, sesame oil, soy sauce and minced ginger in a large bowl. Add the sugar snap peas and the air-fried carrots to the honey mixture, toss to coat and return everything to the air fryer basket.
4. Turn up the temperature to 400ºF (204ºC) and air fry for an additional 6 minutes, shaking the basket once during the cooking process.
5. Transfer the carrots and sugar snap peas to a serving bowl. Pour the sauce from the bottom of the cooker over the vegetables and sprinkle sesame seeds over top. Serve immediately.

Balsamic Pearl Onions with Basil

Prep time: 5 minutes | Cook time: 10 minutes | Serves 2 to 4

- 1 pound (454 g) fresh pearl onions
- 1 tablespoon olive oil
- Salt and freshly ground black pepper
- 1 teaspoon high quality aged
- balsamic vinegar
- 1 tablespoon chopped fresh basil leaves (or mint)

1. Preheat the air fryer to 400ºF (204ºC).
2. Decide whether you want to peel the onions before or after they cook. Peeling them ahead of time is a little more laborious. Peeling after they cook is easier, but a little messier since the onions are hot and you may discard more of the onion than you'd like to. If you opt to peel them first, trim the tiny root of the onions off and pinch off any loose papery skins. (It's ok if there are some skins left on the onions.) Toss the pearl onions with the olive oil, salt and freshly ground black pepper.
3. Air fry for 10 minutes, shaking the basket a couple of times during the cooking process. (If your pearl onions are very large, you may need to add a couple of minutes to this cooking time.)
4. Let the onions cool slightly and then slip off any remaining skins.
5. Toss the onions with the balsamic vinegar and basil and serve.

Parsley Shiitake Mushrooms

Prep time: 10 minutes | Cook time: 5 minutes | Serves 4

- 8 ounces (227 g) shiitake mushrooms, stems removed and caps roughly chopped
- 1 tablespoon olive oil
- ½ teaspoon salt
- Freshly ground black pepper
- 1 teaspoon chopped fresh thyme leaves
- 1 teaspoon chopped fresh oregano
- 1 tablespoon chopped fresh parsley

1. Preheat the air fryer to 400ºF (204ºC).
2. Toss the mushrooms with the olive oil, salt, pepper, thyme and oregano. Air fry for 5 minutes, shaking the basket once or twice during the cooking process. The mushrooms will still be somewhat chewy with a meaty texture. If you'd like them a little more tender, add a couple of minutes to this cooking time.
3. Once cooked, add the parsley to the mushrooms and toss. Season again to taste and serve.

Sesame Cauliflower Rice and Peas

Prep time: 15 minutes | Cook time: 20 minutes | Serves 5

- 2½ cups riced cauliflower
- 2 teaspoons sesame oil, divided
- 1 medium green bell pepper, chopped
- 1 cup peas
- 1 cup diced carrots
- ½ cup chopped onion
- Salt
- Pepper
- 1 tablespoon soy sauce
- 2 medium eggs, scrambled

1. If you choose to make your own riced cauliflower, grate the head of cauliflower using the medium-size holes of a cheese grater. Or you can cut the head of cauliflower into florets and pulse in a food processor until it has the appearance of rice.
2. Coat the bottom of a barrel pan with 1 teaspoon of sesame oil.
3. In a large bowl, combine the riced cauliflower, green bell pepper, peas, carrots, and onion. Drizzle the remaining 1 teaspoon of sesame oil over the vegetables and stir. Add salt and pepper to taste.
4. Transfer the mixture to the barrel pan. Cook at 375ºF (191ºC) for 10 minutes.
5. Remove the barrel pan. Drizzle the soy sauce all over and add the scrambled eggs. Stir to combine.
6. Serve warm.

Ratatouille Vegetables with Basil

Prep time: 15 minutes | Cook time: 15 minutes | Serves 2 to 4

- 1 baby or Japanese eggplant, cut into 1½-inch cubes
- 1 red pepper, cut into 1-inch chunks
- 1 yellow pepper, cut into 1-inch chunks
- 1 zucchini, cut into 1-inch chunks
- 1 clove garlic, minced
- ½ teaspoon dried basil
- 1 tablespoon olive oil
- Salt and freshly ground black pepper
- ¼ cup sliced sun-dried tomatoes in oil
- 2 tablespoons chopped fresh basil

1. Preheat the air fryer to 400ºF (204ºC).
2. Toss the eggplant, peppers and zucchini with the garlic, dried basil, olive oil, salt and freshly ground black pepper.
3. Air fry the vegetables at 400ºF (204ºC) for 15 minutes, shaking the basket a few times during the cooking process to redistribute the ingredients.
4. As soon as the vegetables are tender, toss them with the sliced sun-dried tomatoes and fresh basil and serve.

Chickpea and Curried Cauliflower Salad

Prep time: 20 minutes | Cook time: 23 minutes | Serves 4

- 3½ tablespoons extra-virgin olive oil
- 1½ teaspoons curry powder
- Salt and pepper
- 1 head cauliflower, cored and cut into 1½-inch florets
- ¼ cup plain Greek yogurt
- 2 tablespoons chopped fresh cilantro
- 1½ teaspoons lime juice
- 1 garlic clove, minced
- 1 (15-ounce / 425-g) can chickpeas, rinsed
- 3 ounces (85 g) seedless red grapes, halved
- ¼ cup roasted cashews, chopped

1. Whisk 1½ tablespoons oil, curry powder, ⅛ teaspoon salt, and ⅛ teaspoon pepper together in medium bowl. Add cauliflower and toss to coat; transfer to air fryer basket. Place basket in air fryer and set temperature to 400ºF (204ºC). Cook cauliflower until tender and golden at edges, 23 to 25 minutes, tossing halfway through cooking.
2. Set cauliflower aside to cool slightly. Meanwhile, whisk yogurt, 1 tablespoon cilantro, lime juice, garlic, ⅛ teaspoon salt, ⅛ teaspoon pepper, and remaining 2 tablespoons oil together in serving bowl. Add cooled cauliflower and chickpeas and toss to coat. Season with salt and pepper to taste. Sprinkle with grapes, cashews, and remaining 1 tablespoon cilantro. Serve.

Green Beans with Sun-Dried Tomatoes

Prep time: 15 minutes | Cook time: 12 minutes | Serves 4

- 1 pound (454 g) green beans, trimmed and halved
- 2 teaspoons extra-virgin olive oil
- Salt and pepper
- ½ cup torn fresh basil
- ⅓ cup oil-packed sun-dried
- tomatoes, rinsed, patted dry, and chopped
- 1 tablespoon lemon juice
- 2 ounces (57 g) goat cheese, crumbled
- ¼ cup roasted sunflower seeds

1. Toss green beans with 1 teaspoon oil, ⅛ teaspoon salt, and ⅛ teaspoon pepper in bowl; transfer to air fryer basket. Place basket in air fryer and set temperature to 400ºF (204ºC). Cook green beans until crisp-tender, 12 to 15 minutes, tossing halfway through cooking.
2. Toss green beans with remaining 1 teaspoon oil, basil, sun-dried tomatoes, and lemon juice in large bowl. Season with salt and pepper to taste. Transfer to serving dish and sprinkle with goat cheese and sunflower seeds. Serve.

Balsamic Summer Vegetables with Basil

Prep time: 10 minutes | Cook time: 37 minutes | Serves 2

- 1 cup balsamic vinegar
- 1 zucchini, sliced
- 1 yellow squash, sliced
- 2 tablespoons olive oil
- 1 clove garlic, minced
- ½ teaspoon Italian seasoning
- Salt and freshly ground black pepper
- ½ cup cherry tomatoes, halved
- 2 ounces (57 g) crumbled goat cheese
- 2 tablespoons chopped fresh basil, plus more leaves for garnish

1. Place the balsamic vinegar in a small saucepot on the stovetop. Bring the vinegar to a boil, lower the heat and simmer uncovered for 20 minutes, until the mixture reduces and thickens. Set aside to cool.
2. Preheat the air fryer to 390ºF (199ºC).
3. Combine the zucchini and yellow squash in a large bowl. Add the olive oil, minced garlic, Italian seasoning, salt and pepper and toss to coat.
4. Air fry the vegetables at 390ºF (199ºC) for 10 minutes, shaking the basket several times during the cooking process. Add the cherry tomatoes and continue to air fry for another 5 minutes. Sprinkle the goat cheese over the vegetables and air fry for 2 more minutes.
5. Transfer the vegetables to a serving dish, drizzle with the balsamic reduction and season with freshly ground black pepper. Garnish with the fresh basil leaves.

Sage Butternut Squash with Hazelnuts

Prep time: 15 minutes | Cook time: 30 minutes | Serves 4

- 2 tablespoons cashew butter
- 1 tablespoon minced fresh sage
- 1 teaspoon lemon juice
- Salt and pepper
- 2 pounds (907 g) butternut squash,
- peeled, seeded, and cut into 1-inch pieces
- $1/3$ cup skinned raw hazelnuts, chopped coarse

1. Microwave butter and sage in large bowl at 50 percent power, stirring occasionally, about 1 minute. Transfer 1 tablespoon butter mixture to small bowl, then stir in lemon juice and ⅛ teaspoon salt; set aside. Add squash, ¼ teaspoon salt, and ⅛ teaspoon pepper to remaining butter mixture and toss to coat.
2. Place squash in air fryer basket. Place basket in air fryer, set temperature to 400ºF (204ºC), and cook for 15 minutes. Stir in hazelnuts and cook until squash is tender and well browned, 15 to 20 minutes, tossing halfway through cooking.
3. Transfer squash mixture to clean large bowl; toss with reserved butter mixture. Season with salt and pepper to taste. Serve.

Broccoli and Carrot Medley

Prep time: 5 minutes | Cook time: 15 minutes | Serves 4

- 1 head broccoli, chopped
- 2 medium carrots, cut into 1-inch pieces
- Salt
- Pepper
- Cooking oil
- 1 zucchini, cut into 1-inch chunks
- 1 medium red bell pepper, seeded and thinly sliced

1. In a large bowl, combine the broccoli and carrots. Season with salt and pepper to taste. Spray with cooking oil.
2. Transfer the broccoli and carrots to the air fryer basket. Cook at 390ºF (199ºC) for 6 minutes.
3. Place the zucchini and red pepper in the bowl. Season with salt and pepper to taste. Spray with cooking oil.
4. Add the zucchini and red pepper to the broccoli and carrots in the air fryer basket. Cook for 6 minutes.
5. Cool before serving.

Eggplant Bharta with Cilantro

Prep time: 10 minutes | Cook time: 20 minutes | Serves 4

- 1 medium eggplant
- 2 tablespoons vegetable oil
- ½ cup finely minced onion
- ½ cup finely chopped fresh tomato
- 2 tablespoons fresh lemon juice
- 2 tablespoons chopped fresh cilantro
- ½ teaspoon kosher salt
- ⅛ teaspoon cayenne pepper

1. Rub the eggplant all over with the vegetable oil. Place the eggplant in the air fryer basket. Set the air fryer to 400ºF (204ºC) for 20 minutes, or until the eggplant skin is blistered and charred.
2. Transfer the eggplant to a resealable plastic bag, seal, and set aside for 15 to 20 minutes (the eggplant will finish cooking in the residual heat trapped in the bag).
3. Transfer the eggplant to a large bowl. Peel off and discard the charred skin. Roughly mash the eggplant flesh. Add the onion, tomato, lemon juice, cilantro, salt, and cayenne. Stir to combine.

Mozzarella Veggie-Stuffed Peppers

Prep time: 15 minutes | Cook time: 15 minutes | Serves 4

- 4 large red bell peppers
- 1½ cups cooked rice
- ¼ cup chopped onion
- ¼ cup sliced mushrooms
- ¾ cup marinara sauce
- Salt
- Pepper
- ¾ cup shredded mozzarella cheese

1. Boil a large pot of water over high heat.
2. Cut off the tops of the peppers. You can save the tops for decorative plating after you have cooked the peppers. Remove the seeds and hollow out the inside of the peppers.
3. Add the peppers to the boiling water for 5 minutes. Remove and allow them to cool for 3 to 4 minutes.
4. In a large bowl, combine the cooked rice, onion, mushrooms, and marinara sauce. Season with salt and pepper to taste.
5. Stuff the peppers with the rice mixture. Sprinkle the mozzarella cheese on top of the peppers.
6. Place the stuffed peppers in the air fryer. Cook at 350ºF (177ºC) for 10 minutes.
7. Cool before serving.

Cauliflower Steaks with Tahini-Lemon Sauce

Prep time: 20 minutes | Cook time: 15 to 17 minutes | Serves 3 to 4

Tahini Sauce:
- ½ cup tahini
- ½ cup freshly squeezed lemon juice

- 2 tablespoons extra-virgin olive oil
- ½ cup warm water

Cauliflower Steaks:
- 2 heads cauliflower
- 1 cup whole wheat flour
- 2 cups whole wheat bread crumbs
- 2 teaspoons thyme
- 2 teaspoons oregano
- 1 teaspoon kosher salt

- 1 teaspoon black pepper
- 2 eggs beaten with 2 tablespoons water
- Vegetable oil for spraying
- ¼ cup chopped flat-leaf parsley
- Lemon wedges for serving

1. To make the tahini sauce, combine the tahini, lemon juice, and olive oil in a small bowl. Slowly whisk in the water until you reach the desired consistency, (You may not need the entire ½ cup.) Set aside.
2. To make the cauliflower steaks, remove the leaves and trim the stems of the cauliflower, leaving the cores intact. Stand the cauliflower on a cutting board. Using a large knife, slice off the rounded sides of the cauliflower, leaving the middle section still attached to the core. Slice this middle section into 2 or 3 flat "steaks," depending on the size of the cauliflower, 1 to 1½ inches (2.5 to 4 cm) thick.
3. Place the flour in a shallow dish or pie plate. In a separate shallow dish, combine the bread crumbs, thyme, oregano, salt, and pepper. Dredge 2 of the cauliflower steaks first in the flour, then the egg mixture, and finally the panko mixture, coating both sides. Remove to a plate.
4. Preheat the air fryer to 375ºF (191ºC). Spray both sides of the cauliflower steaks with oil and place in the basket of the air fryer. Cook for 15 to 17 minutes, flipping the steaks once halfway through, until the cauliflower is fork-tender and the breading is browned and crispy. Repeat with the remaining steaks. Drizzle tahini sauce over the steaks and serve with parsley and lemon wedges.

Air Fryer Corn on the Cob

Prep time: 10 minutes | Cook time: 10 minutes | Serves 4

- 4 ears corn, shucked and halved crosswise
- 1 tablespoon extra-virgin olive oil

- Salt
- Pepper

1. Place the corn in a large bowl. Coat with the olive oil and season with salt and pepper to taste.
2. Place the corn in the air fryer. Cook at 390ºF (199ºC) for 6 minutes.
3. Cool before serving.

Parmesan-Lemon Asparagus

Prep time: 5 minutes | Cook time: 5 minutes | Serves 2

- 1 bunch asparagus, stems trimmed
- 1 teaspoon olive oil
- Salt and freshly ground black pepper
- ¼ cup coarsely grated Parmesan cheese
- ½ lemon

1. Preheat the air fryer to 400ºF (204ºC).
2. Toss the asparagus with the oil and season with salt and freshly ground black pepper.
3. Transfer the asparagus to the air fryer basket and air fry at 400ºF (204ºC) for 5 minutes, shaking the basket to turn the asparagus once or twice during the cooking process.
4. When the asparagus is cooked to your liking, sprinkle the asparagus generously with the Parmesan cheese and close the air fryer drawer again. Let the asparagus sit for 1 minute in the turned-off air fryer. Then, remove the asparagus, transfer it to a serving dish and finish with a grind of black pepper and a squeeze of lemon juice.

Parmesan Zucchini Fries

Prep time: 20 minutes | Cook time: 16 to 20 minutes | Serves 4

- 1 cup yellow cornmeal
- 1 teaspoon Creole Seasoning
- 1 teaspoon salt
- ½ teaspoon freshly ground black pepper
- 2 large eggs, beaten
- ¼ cup grated Parmesan cheese
- 1½ cups whole wheat bread crumbs
- 2 zucchini, peeled and cut into 1-inch-thick strips
- 1 to 2 tablespoons oil

1. In a shallow dish, whisk the cornmeal, Creole Seasoning, salt, and pepper until blended. Place the beaten eggs in a second shallow bowl, and stir together the Parmesan cheese and bread crumbs in a third bowl.
2. One at a time, dip the zucchini into the cornmeal, the beaten eggs, and the bread crumbs, coating thoroughly.
3. Preheat the air fryer to 350ºF (177ºC). Line the air fryer tray with parchment paper.
4. Place half the zucchini fries on the parchment and spritz with oil.
5. Cook for 4 minutes. Shake the basket, spritz the fries with oil, and cook for 4 to 6 minutes more until lightly browned and crispy. Repeat with the remaining fries.

Lettuce and Tofu Salad

Prep time: 15 minutes | Cook time: 15 minutes | Serves 2

For the Tofu:
- 1 tablespoon soy sauce
- 1 tablespoon vegetable oil
- 1 teaspoon minced fresh ginger
- 1 teaspoon minced garlic
- 8 ounces (227 g) extra-firm tofu, drained and cubed

For the Salad:
- ¼ cup rice vinegar
- 1 tablespoon honey
- 1 teaspoon salt
- 1 teaspoon black pepper
- ¼ cup sliced scallions
- 1 cup julienned cucumber
- 1 cup julienned red onion
- 1 cup julienned carrots
- 6 butter lettuce leaves

1. For the tofu: In a small bowl, whisk together the soy sauce, vegetable oil, ginger, and garlic. Add the tofu and mix gently. Let stand at room temperature for 10 minutes.
2. Arrange the tofu in a single layer in the air fryer basket. Set the air fryer to 400ºF (204ºC) for 15 minutes, shaking halfway through the cooking time.
3. Meanwhile, for the salad: In a large bowl, whisk together the vinegar, honey, salt, pepper, and scallions. Add the cucumber, onion, and carrots and toss to combine. Set aside to marinate while the tofu cooks.
4. To serve, arrange three lettuce leaves on each of two plates. Pile the marinated vegetables (and marinade) on the lettuce. Divide the tofu between the plates and serve.

Feta Veggie-Stuffed Portobellos

Prep time: 20 minutes | Cook time: 10 to 12 minutes | Serves 4

- 4 large portobello mushroom caps (about 3 ounces / 85 g each)
- Olive oil spray
- Kosher salt
- 2 medium plum tomatoes, chopped
- 1 cup baby spinach, roughly chopped
- ¾ cup crumbled feta cheese
- 1 shallot, chopped
- 1 large garlic clove, minced
- ¼ cup chopped fresh basil
- 2 tablespoons whole wheat bread crumbs
- 1 tablespoon chopped fresh oregano
- 1 tablespoon freshly grated Parmesan cheese
- ⅛ teaspoon freshly ground black pepper
- 1 tablespoon olive oil
- Balsamic glaze (optional), for drizzling

1. Use a small metal spoon to carefully scrape the black gills out of each mushroom cap. Spray both sides of the mushrooms with olive oil and season with a pinch of salt.
2. In a medium bowl, combine the tomatoes, spinach, feta, shallot, garlic, basil, bread crumbs, oregano, Parmesan, ¼ teaspoon salt, pepper, and olive oil and mix well. Carefully fill the inside of each mushroom cap with the mixture.
3. Preheat the air fryer to 370°F (188°C).
4. Working in batches, arrange a single layer of the stuffed mushrooms in the air fryer basket. Cook for 10 to 12 minutes, until the mushrooms are tender and the top is golden. Use a flexible spatula to carefully remove the mushrooms from the basket and transfer to a serving dish. Drizzle the balsamic glaze (if using) over the mushrooms and serve.

Scallion Tofu

Prep time: 10 minutes | Cook time: 12 t0 14 minutes | Serves 4

- 14 ounces (397 g) extra-firm tofu, preferably silken
- ¼ cup plus 2 tablespoons cornstarch
- 1½ teaspoons fine sea salt
- 1 teaspoon freshly ground black
- pepper
- Vegetable oil for spraying
- 2 scallions, white and green parts only, sliced

1. Place the tofu on a paper towel-lined plate. Cover with another plate and place something heavy, such as a can from your pantry, on top of the plate. Press the tofu in this manner for 20 minutes to remove some of the liquid.
2. When the tofu has drained, cut it into 1-inch (2.5 cm) cubes. Place the cornstarch, salt, and pepper in a medium bowl. Place the tofu cubes in the bowl and toss them in the cornstarch mixture until they are coated on all sides. Remove half of the tofu cubes from the bowl, leaving the other half in the cornstarch, and shake each one to remove any excess cornstarch. Place the coated tofu cubes on a plate.
3. Spray the basket of the air fryer with oil. Arrange half of the tofu cubes in a single layer in the basket, taking care not to crowd them. Spray the cubes well with oil. Cook at 400°F (204°C) for 12 to 14 minutes, shaking the basket once or twice during cooking to toss the cubes. If you notice cornstarch on the outside of the cubes that is not browning, spray those areas with additional oil.
4. When the first batch of tofu cubes is light golden in color on all sides and there are no visible patches of cornstarch remaining, remove to a plate. Remove the second batch of tofu cubes from the cornstarch and cook in the same manner.
5. Serve warm garnished with scallions. (The tofu will lose the crispy texture as it cools.)

Lemon Spinach Rigatoni

Prep time: 10 minutes | Cook time: 13 minutes | Serves 2 to 3

- 1 red onion, rough chopped into large chunks
- 2 teaspoons olive oil, divided
- 1 bulb fennel, sliced ¼-inch thick
- ¾ cup ricotta cheese
- 1½ teaspoons finely chopped lemon
- zest, plus more for garnish
- 1 teaspoon lemon juice
- Salt and freshly ground black pepper
- 8 ounces (227 g) dried rigatoni pasta
- 3 cups baby spinach leaves

1. Bring a large stockpot of salted water to a boil on the stovetop and preheat the air fryer to 400ºF (204ºC).
2. While the water is coming to a boil, toss the chopped onion in 1 teaspoon of olive oil and transfer to the air fryer basket. Air fry at 400ºF (204ºC) for 5 minutes. Toss the sliced fennel with 1 teaspoon of olive oil and add this to the air fryer basket with the onions. Continue to air fry at 400ºF (204ºC) for 8 minutes, shaking the basket a few times during the cooking process.
3. Combine the ricotta cheese, lemon zest and juice, ¼ teaspoon of salt and freshly ground black pepper in a bowl and stir until smooth.
4. Add the dried rigatoni to the boiling water and cook according to the package directions. When the pasta is cooked al dente, reserve one cup of the pasta water and drain the pasta into a colander.
5. Place the spinach in a serving bowl and immediately transfer the hot pasta to the bowl, wilting the spinach. Add the roasted onions and fennel and toss together. Add a little pasta water to the dish if it needs moistening. Then, dollop the lemon pepper ricotta cheese on top and nestle it into the hot pasta. Garnish with more lemon zest if desired.

Sriracha Green Bean and Tofu Fry

Prep time: 25 minutes | Cook time: 17 minutes | Serves 4 to 6

- 4 teaspoons canola oil, divided
- 2 tablespoons rice wine vinegar
- 1 tablespoon sriracha chili sauce
- ¼ cup soy sauce
- ½ teaspoon toasted sesame oil
- 1 teaspoon minced garlic
- 1 tablespoon minced fresh ginger
- 8 ounces (227 g) extra firm tofu
- ½ cup vegetable stock or water
- 1 tablespoon honey
- 1 tablespoon cornstarch
- ½ red onion, chopped
- 1 red or yellow bell pepper, chopped
- 1 cup green beans, cut into 2-inch lengths
- 4 ounces (113 g) mushrooms, sliced
- 2 scallions, sliced
- 2 tablespoons fresh cilantro leaves
- 2 teaspoons toasted sesame seeds

1. Combine 1 tablespoon of the oil, vinegar, sriracha sauce, soy sauce, sesame oil, garlic and ginger in a small bowl. Cut the tofu into bite-sized cubes and toss the tofu in with the marinade while you prepare the other vegetables. When you are ready to start cooking, remove the tofu from the marinade and set it aside. Add the water, honey and cornstarch to the marinade and bring to a simmer on the stovetop, just until the sauce thickens. Set the sauce aside.
2. Preheat the air fryer to 400ºF (204ºC).
3. Toss the onion, pepper, green beans and mushrooms in a bowl with a little canola oil and season with salt. Air fry at 400ºF (204ºC) for 10 to 12 minutes, shaking the basket and tossing the vegetables every few minutes. When the vegetables are cooked to your preferred doneness, remove them from the air fryer and set aside.
4. Add the tofu to the air fryer basket and air fry at 400ºF (204ºC) for 6 minutes, shaking the basket a few times during the cooking process. Add the vegetables back to the basket and air fry for another minute. Transfer the vegetables and tofu to a large bowl, add the scallions and cilantro leaves and toss with the sauce. Serve over rice with sesame seeds sprinkled on top.

Asparagus and Broccoli Green Curry

Prep time: 20 minutes | Cook time: 16 minutes | Serves 4

- 1 (13-ounce / 369-g) can unsweetened coconut milk
- 3 tablespoons green curry paste
- 1 tablespoon soy sauce
- 1 tablespoon rice wine vinegar
- 1 teaspoon honey
- 1 teaspoon minced fresh ginger
- ½ onion, chopped
- 3 carrots, sliced
- 1 red bell pepper, chopped
- Olive oil
- 10 stalks of asparagus, cut into 2-inch pieces
- 3 cups broccoli florets
- Basmati rice for serving
- Fresh cilantro
- Crushed red pepper flakes (optional)

1. Combine the coconut milk, green curry paste, soy sauce, rice wine vinegar, honey and ginger in a medium saucepan and bring to a boil on the stovetop. Reduce the heat and simmer for 20 minutes while you cook the vegetables. Set aside.
2. Preheat the air fryer to 400ºF (204ºC).
3. Toss the onion, carrots, and red pepper together with a little olive oil and transfer the vegetables to the air fryer basket. Air fry at 400ºF (204ºC) for 10 minutes, shaking the basket a few times during the cooking process. Add the asparagus and broccoli florets and air fry for an additional 6 minutes, again shaking the basket for even cooking.
4. When the vegetables are cooked to your liking, toss them with the green curry sauce and serve in bowls over basmati rice. Garnish with fresh chopped cilantro and crushed red pepper flakes.

Masala-Glazed Potato Chips

Prep time: 20 minutes | Cook time: 34 to 36 minutes | Serves 2

- 2 large russet potatoes
- 3 tablespoons olive oil
- 3 cloves garlic, minced
- 1 piece fresh ginger, peeled and grated
- ½ yellow onion, diced
- 2 teaspoons kosher salt, divided
- 1 serrano pepper, seeded and minced
- 1½ teaspoons garam masala
- ½ teaspoon cumin
- ¼ teaspoon turmeric
- 1 tablespoon tomato paste
- 2 medium tomatoes, diced
- 2 teaspoons vegetable oil
- Juice of 1 lemon
- 2 tablespoons chopped cilantro
- 2 tablespoons crumbly hard cheese such as a mild feta, paneer, or queso fresco

1. Peel the potatoes and cut them into ¼-inch (6 mm) slices. Cut each slice into 4 or 5 thick fries. (Halve any especially long pieces. You're looking for fries the size of your finger.) Place the cut potatoes into a bowl of cold water and let them soak for at least 30 minutes to get rid of excess starch.
2. While the potatoes are soaking, make the masala. Heat the oil in a large, deep skillet over medium heat. Add the garlic and ginger and cook for 1 minute, stirring. Add the onion and season with 1 teaspoon of the salt. Sauté the onion, stirring, for 5 minutes. Add the serrano pepper and spices and sauté for 3 additional minutes.
3. Add the tomato paste and diced tomatoes to the skillet and stir to combine. Sauté the tomatoes until they begin to break down and form a sauce, about 5 minutes. Remove the skillet from the heat and set aside.
4. Preheat the air fryer to 400ºF (204ºC). Drain the potatoes and dry them well. Toss the potatoes with the oil and remaining teaspoon of salt. Arrange the potatoes in a single layer in the basket of the air fryer. (Depending on the size of your machine, you may have to work in 2 batches. Do not overcrowd the basket.) Cook for 10 minutes. Open the air fryer and shake the basket to redistribute the potatoes. Cook for an additional 10 to 12 minutes until all the potatoes are browned and crisp.
5. Place the fries in the skillet with the masala sauce and add the lemon juice. Toss to coat with the sauce and cook over medium heat for a few minutes until warmed through.
6. Arrange the masala fries on a platter and garnish with chopped cilantro and crumbled cheese. Serve immediately.

Broccoli and Farro Bowls

Prep time: 20 minutes | Cook time: 16 minutes | Makes 2 grain bowls

Creamy Herb Dressing:
- ½ cup plain Greek yogurt
- ½ cup fresh cilantro or basil leaves
- 2 tablespoons extra-virgin olive oil
- 1 clove garlic, peeled
- Juice of 1 lemon
- ½ teaspoon kosher salt
- ½ teaspoon cumin

Grain Bowls:
- 1 cup diced sweet potatoes
- 2 cups broccoli florets
- 1 teaspoon kosher salt, divided
- 2 teaspoons extra-virgin olive oil, divided
- 2 cups cooked and cooled pearled farro
- ½ small red onion, thinly sliced
- 1 small avocado, pitted and diced
- Kosher salt and pepper to taste

1. To make the Creamy Herb Dressing, combine all dressing ingredients in a blender. Blend on medium speed until completely combined and smooth. If the dressing is too thick, add 1 to 2 tablespoons of water.
2. Combine the sweet potatoes, broccoli, and ½ teaspoon of the salt in a bowl with 1 teaspoon of the olive oil and toss to combine. Arrange the vegetables in a single layer in the basket of the air fryer and cook at 350ºF (177ºC) until the potatoes are golden brown and the broccoli is tender and starting to brown on the tops, about 8 minutes. Transfer the vegetables to a platter and keep warm.
3. Drizzle the cooked farro with the remaining teaspoon of olive oil and salt and toss to combine. Cut a small piece of parchment paper into a round to cover the bottom of the air fryer basket to prevent the farro grains from slipping through the basket holes. Add the farro to the basket and cook at 350ºF (177ºC) for 8 minutes, tossing gently halfway through to ensure that each grain is crisping, until the farro is crisp and golden.
4. Divide the farro between 2 bowls and top each with the sweet potatoes, broccoli, red onion, and avocado. Season with salt and pepper and drizzle with Creamy Herb Dressing. Serve warm or at room temperature.

CHAPTER 5

BEANS AND GRAINS

Goat Cheese and Red Lentil Stuffed Tomatoes

Prep time: 10 minutes | Cook time: 15 minutes | Serves 4

- 4 tomatoes
- ½ cup cooked red lentils
- 1 garlic clove, minced
- 1 tablespoon minced red onion
- 4 basil leaves, minced
- ¼ teaspoon salt
- ¼ teaspoon black pepper
- 4 ounces (113 g) goat cheese
- 2 tablespoons shredded Parmesan cheese

1. Preheat the air fryer to 380ºF (193ºC).
2. Slice the top off of each tomato.
3. Using a knife and spoon, cut and scoop out half of the flesh inside of the tomato. Place it into a medium bowl.
4. To the bowl with the tomato, add the cooked lentils, garlic, onion, basil, salt, pepper, and goat cheese. Stir until well combined.
5. Spoon the filling into the scooped-out cavity of each of the tomatoes, then top each one with ½ tablespoon of shredded Parmesan cheese.
6. Place the tomatoes in a single layer in the air fryer basket and bake for 15 minutes.

Green Peas and Cauliflower Bake

Prep time: 5 minutes | Cook time: 25 minutes | Serves 8

- 1 cup cauliflower florets, fresh or frozen
- ½ white onion, roughly chopped
- 2 tablespoons olive oil
- ½ cup unsweetened almond milk
- 3 cups green peas, fresh or frozen
- 3 garlic cloves, minced
- 2 tablespoons fresh thyme leaves, chopped
- 1 teaspoon fresh rosemary leaves, chopped
- ½ teaspoon salt
- ½ teaspoon black pepper
- Shredded Parmesan cheese, for garnish
- Fresh parsley, for garnish

1. Preheat the air fryer to 380ºF (193ºC).
2. In a large bowl, combine the cauliflower florets and onion with the olive oil and toss well to coat.
3. Put the cauliflower-and-onion mixture into the air fryer basket in an even layer and bake for 15 minutes.
4. Transfer the cauliflower and onion to a food processor. Add the almond milk and pulse until smooth.
5. In a medium saucepan, combine the cauliflower puree, peas, garlic, thyme, rosemary, salt, and pepper and mix well. Cook over medium heat for an additional 10 minutes, stirring regularly.
6. Serve with a sprinkle of Parmesan cheese and chopped fresh parsley.

Balsamic Two-Beans with Dill

Prep time: 5 minutes | Cook time: 30 minutes | Serves 4

- Olive oil cooking spray
- 1 (15-ounce / 425-g) can cannellini beans, drained and rinsed
- 1 (15-ounce / 425-g) can great northern beans, drained and rinsed
- ½ yellow onion, diced
- 1 (8-ounce / 227-g) can tomato sauce
- 1½ tablespoons honey
- ¼ cup olive oil
- 2 garlic cloves, minced
- 2 tablespoons chopped fresh dill
- ½ teaspoon salt
- ½ teaspoon black pepper
- 1 bay leaf
- 1 tablespoon balsamic vinegar
- 2 ounces (57 g) feta cheese, crumbled, for serving

1. Preheat the air fryer to 360°F (182°C). Lightly coat the inside of a 5-cup capacity casserole dish with olive oil cooking spray. (The shape of the casserole dish will depend upon the size of the air fryer, but it needs to be able to hold at least 5 cups.)
2. In a large bowl, combine all ingredients except the feta cheese and stir until well combined.
3. Pour the bean mixture into the prepared casserole dish.
4. Bake in the air fryer for 30 minutes.
5. Remove from the air fryer and remove and discard the bay leaf. Sprinkle crumbled feta over the top before serving.

Green Lentil and Brown Rice Balls

Prep time: 5 minutes | Cook time: 11 minutes | Serves 6

- ½ cup cooked green lentils
- 2 garlic cloves, minced
- ¼ white onion, minced
- ¼ cup parsley leaves
- 5 basil leaves
- 1 cup cooked brown rice
- 1 tablespoon lemon juice
- 1 tablespoon olive oil
- ½ teaspoon salt

1. Preheat the air fryer to 380°F (193°C).
2. In a food processor, pulse the cooked lentils with the garlic, onion, parsley, and basil until mostly smooth. (You will want some bits of lentils in the mixture.)
3. Pour the lentil mixture into a large bowl, and stir in brown rice, lemon juice, olive oil, and salt. Stir until well combined.
4. Form the rice mixture into 1-inch balls. Place the rice balls in a single layer in the air fryer basket, making sure that they don't touch each other.
5. Fry for 6 minutes. Turn the rice balls and then fry for an additional 4 to 5 minutes, or until browned on all sides.

White Beans with Garlic and Peppers

Prep time: 5 minutes | Cook time: 15 minutes | Serves 4

- Olive oil cooking spray
- 2 (15-ounce / 425-g) cans white beans, or cannellini beans, drained and rinsed
- 1 red bell pepper, diced
- ½ red onion, diced
- 3 garlic cloves, minced
- 1 tablespoon olive oil
- ¼ to ½ teaspoon salt
- ½ teaspoon black pepper
- 1 rosemary sprig
- 1 bay leaf

1. Preheat the air fryer to 360°F (182°C). Lightly coat the inside of a 5-cup capacity casserole dish with olive oil cooking spray. (The shape of the casserole dish will depend upon the size of the air fryer, but it needs to be able to hold at least 5 cups.)
2. In a large bowl, combine the beans, bell pepper, onion, garlic, olive oil, salt, and pepper.
3. Pour the bean mixture into the prepared casserole dish, place the rosemary and bay leaf on top, and then place the casserole dish into the air fryer.
4. Roast for 15 minutes.
5. Remove the rosemary and bay leaves, then stir well before serving.

Parmesan Farro Risotto with Sage

Prep time: 5 minutes | Cook time: 35 minutes | Serves 6

- Olive oil cooking spray
- 1½ cups uncooked farro
- 2½ cups chicken broth
- 1 cup tomato sauce
- 1 yellow onion, diced
- 3 garlic cloves, minced
- 1 tablespoon fresh sage, chopped
- ½ teaspoon salt
- 2 tablespoons olive oil
- 1 cup Parmesan cheese, grated, divided

1. Preheat the air fryer to 380°F (193°C). Lightly coat the inside of a 5-cup capacity casserole dish with olive oil cooking spray. (The shape of the casserole dish will depend upon the size of the air fryer, but it needs to be able to hold at least 5 cups.)
2. In a large bowl, combine the farro, broth, tomato sauce, onion, garlic, sage, salt, olive oil, and ½ cup of the Parmesan.
3. Pour the farro mixture into the prepared casserole dish and cover with aluminum foil.
4. Bake for 20 minutes, then uncover and stir. Sprinkle the remaining ½ cup Parmesan over the top and bake for 15 minutes more.
5. Stir well before serving.

Garlic Pinto Bean

Prep time: 5 minutes | Cook time: 8 minutes | Serves 2

- 1 (15-ounce / 425-g) can pinto beans, drained
- ¼ cup tomato sauce
- 2 tablespoons nutritional yeast
- 2 large garlic cloves, pressed or minced
- ½ teaspoon dried oregano
- ½ teaspoon cumin
- ¼ teaspoon sea salt
- ⅛ teaspoon freshly ground black pepper
- Cooking oil spray

1. In a medium bowl, stir together the beans, tomato sauce, nutritional yeast, garlic, oregano, cumin, salt, and pepper until well combined.
2. Spray the 6-inch round, 2-inch deep baking pan with oil and pour the bean mixture into it. Bake at 390ºF (199ºC) for 4 minutes. Remove, stir well, and bake for another 4 minutes, or until the mixture has thickened and is heated through. It will most likely form a little crust on top and be lightly browned in spots. Serve hot. This will keep, refrigerated in an airtight container, for up to a week.

Pearl Barley and Mushroom Pilaf

Prep time: 5 minutes | Cook time: 37 minutes | Serves 4

- Olive oil cooking spray
- 2 tablespoons olive oil
- 8 ounces (227 g) button mushrooms, diced
- ½ yellow onion, diced
- 2 garlic cloves, minced
- 1 cup pearl barley
- 2 cups vegetable broth
- 1 tablespoon fresh thyme, chopped
- ½ teaspoon salt
- ¼ teaspoon smoked paprika
- Fresh parsley, for garnish

1. Preheat the air fryer to 380ºF (193ºC). Lightly coat the inside of a 5-cup capacity casserole dish with olive oil cooking spray. (The shape of the casserole dish will depend upon the size of the air fryer, but it needs to be able to hold at least 5 cups.)
2. In a large skillet, heat the olive oil over medium heat. Add the mushrooms and onion and cook, stirring occasionally, for 5 minutes, or until the mushrooms begin to brown.
3. Add the garlic and cook for an additional 2 minutes. Transfer the vegetables to a large bowl.
4. Add the barley, broth, thyme, salt, and paprika.
5. Pour the barley-and-vegetable mixture into the prepared casserole dish, and place the dish into the air fryer. Bake for 15 minutes.
6. Stir the barley mixture. Reduce the heat to 360ºF (182ºC), then return the barley to the air fryer and bake for 15 minutes more.
7. Remove from the air fryer and let sit for 5 minutes before fluffing with a fork and topping with fresh parsley.

Butter Bean Bake with Tomatoes

Prep time: 5 minutes | Cook time: 30 minutes | Serves 4

- Olive oil cooking spray
- 1 (15-ounce / 425-g) can cooked butter beans, drained and rinsed
- 1 cup diced fresh tomatoes
- ½ tablespoon tomato paste
- 2 garlic cloves, minced
- ½ yellow onion, diced
- ½ teaspoon salt
- ¼ cup olive oil
- ¼ cup fresh parsley, chopped

1. Preheat the air fryer to 380ºF (193ºC). Lightly coat the inside of a 5-cup capacity casserole dish with olive oil cooking spray. (The shape of the casserole dish will depend upon the size of the air fryer, but it needs to be able to hold at least 5 cups.)
2. In a large bowl, combine the butter beans, tomatoes, tomato paste, garlic, onion, salt, and olive oil, mixing until all ingredients are combined.
3. Pour the mixture into the prepared casserole dish and top with the chopped parsley.
4. Bake in the air fryer for 15 minutes. Stir well, then return to the air fryer and bake for 15 minutes more.

Black Bean and Sweet Potato Burgers

Prep time: 10 minutes | Cook time: 10 minutes | Serves 4

- 1 (15-ounce / 425-g) can black beans, drained and rinsed
- 1 cup mashed sweet potato
- ½ teaspoon dried oregano
- ¼ teaspoon dried thyme
- ¼ teaspoon dried marjoram
- 1 garlic clove, minced

For Serving:
- Whole wheat buns or whole wheat pitas
- Plain Greek yogurt
- Avocado

- ¼ teaspoon salt
- ¼ teaspoon black pepper
- 1 tablespoon lemon juice
- 1 cup cooked brown rice
- ¼ to ½ cup whole wheat bread crumbs
- 1 tablespoon olive oil

- Lettuce
- Tomato
- Red onion

1. Preheat the air fryer to 380ºF (193ºC).
2. In a large bowl, use the back of a fork to mash the black beans until there are no large pieces left.
3. Add the mashed sweet potato, oregano, thyme, marjoram, garlic, salt, pepper, and lemon juice, and mix until well combined.

4. Stir in the cooked rice.
5. Add in ¼ cup of the whole wheat bread crumbs and stir. Check to see if the mixture is dry enough to form patties. If it seems too wet and loose, add an additional ¼ cup bread crumbs and stir.
6. Form the dough into 4 patties. Place them into the air fryer basket in a single layer, making sure that they don't touch each other.
7. Brush half of the olive oil onto the patties and bake for 5 minutes.
8. Flip the patties over, brush the other side with the remaining oil, and bake for an additional 4 to 5 minutes.
9. Serve on toasted whole wheat buns or whole wheat pitas with a spoonful of yogurt and avocado, lettuce, tomato, and red onion as desired.

Buckwheat, Potato and Carrot Bake

Prep time: 15 minutes | Cook time: 30 minutes | Serves 6

- Olive oil cooking spray
- 2 large potatoes, cubed
- 2 carrots, sliced
- 1 small rutabaga, cubed
- 2 celery stalks, chopped
- ½ teaspoon smoked paprika
- ¼ cup plus 1 tablespoon olive oil,
  divided
- 2 rosemary sprigs
- 1 cup buckwheat groats
- 2 cups vegetable broth
- 2 garlic cloves, minced
- ½ yellow onion, chopped
- 1 teaspoon salt

1. Preheat the air fryer to 380ºF (193ºC). Lightly coat the inside of a 5-cup capacity casserole dish with olive oil cooking spray. (The shape of the casserole dish will depend upon the size of the air fryer, but it needs to be able to hold at least 5 cups.)
2. In a large bowl, toss the potatoes, carrots, rutabaga, and celery with the paprika and ¼ cup olive oil.
3. Pour the vegetable mixture into the prepared casserole dish and top with the rosemary sprigs. Place the casserole dish into the air fryer and bake for 15 minutes.
4. While the vegetables are cooking, rinse and drain the buckwheat groats.
5. In a medium saucepan over medium-high heat, combine the groats, vegetable broth, garlic, onion, and salt with the remaining 1 tablespoon olive oil. Bring the mixture to a boil, then reduce the heat to low, cover, and cook for 10 to 12 minutes.
6. Remove the casserole dish from the air fryer. Remove the rosemary sprigs and discard. Pour the cooked buckwheat into the dish with the vegetables and stir to combine. Cover with aluminum foil and bake for an additional 15 minutes.
7. Stir before serving.

Red Lentils and Onions with Lemon

Prep time: 10 minutes | Cook time: 45 minutes | Serves 4

- 1 cup red lentils
- 4 cups water
- Cooking oil spray
- 1 medium-size onion, peeled and cut into ¼-inch-thick rings
- Sea salt
- ½ cup kale, stems removed, thinly sliced
- 3 large garlic cloves, pressed or minced
- 2 tablespoons fresh lemon juice
- 2 teaspoons nutritional yeast
- 1 teaspoon sea salt
- 1 teaspoon lemon zest
- ¾ teaspoon freshly ground black pepper

1. In a medium-large pot, bring the lentils and water to a boil over medium-high heat. Reduce the heat to low and simmer, uncovered, for about 30 minutes (or until the lentils have dissolved completely), making sure to stir every 5 minutes or so as they cook (so that the lentils don't stick to the bottom of the pot).
2. While the lentils are cooking, get the rest of your dish together. Spray the air fryer basket with oil and place the onion rings inside, separating them as much as possible. Spray them with the oil and sprinkle with a little salt. Fry at 390°F (199°C) for 5 minutes. Remove the air fryer basket, shake or stir, spray again with oil, and fry for another 5 minutes.
3. Remove the air fryer basket, spray the onions again with oil, and fry for a final 5 minutes or until all the pieces are crisp and browned.
4. To finish the lentils: Add the kale to the hot lentils, and stir very well, as the heat from the lentils will steam the thinly sliced greens. Stir in the garlic, lemon juice, nutritional yeast, salt, zest, and pepper. Stir very well and then distribute evenly in bowls. Top with the crisp onion rings and serve.

Chickpea and Brown Rice Bake

Prep time: 10 minutes | Cook time: 45 minutes | Serves 6

- Olive oil cooking spray
- 1 cup long-grain brown rice
- 2¼ cups chicken stock
- 1 (15½-ounce / 439-g) can chickpeas, drained and rinsed
- ½ cup diced carrot
- ½ cup green peas
- 1 teaspoon ground cumin
- ½ teaspoon ground turmeric
- ½ teaspoon ground ginger
- ½ teaspoon onion powder
- ½ teaspoon salt
- ¼ teaspoon ground cinnamon
- ¼ teaspoon garlic powder
- ¼ teaspoon black pepper
- Fresh parsley, for garnish

1. Preheat the air fryer to 380°F (193°C). Lightly coat the inside of a 5-cup capacity casserole dish with olive oil cooking spray. (The shape of the casserole dish will depend upon the size of the air fryer, but it needs to be able to hold at least 5 cups.)
2. In the casserole dish, combine the rice, stock, chickpeas, carrot, peas, cumin, turmeric, ginger, onion powder, salt, cinnamon, garlic powder, and black pepper. Stir well to combine.
3. Cover loosely with aluminum foil.
4. Place the covered casserole dish into the air fryer and bake for 20 minutes. Remove from the air fryer and stir well.
5. Place the casserole back into the air fryer, uncovered, and bake for 25 minutes more.
6. Fluff with a spoon and sprinkle with fresh chopped parsley before serving.

Red Lentil-Veggie Patties

Prep time: 15 minutes | Cook time: 10 minutes | Serves 4

- 1 cup cooked brown lentils
- ¼ cup fresh parsley leaves
- ½ cup shredded carrots
- ¼ red onion, minced
- ¼ red bell pepper, minced
- 1 jalapeño, seeded and minced
- 2 garlic cloves, minced
- 1 egg

- 2 tablespoons lemon juice
- 2 tablespoons olive oil, divided
- ½ teaspoon onion powder
- ½ teaspoon smoked paprika
- ½ teaspoon dried oregano
- ¼ teaspoon salt
- ¼ teaspoon black pepper
- ½ cup whole wheat bread crumbs

For Serving:
- Whole wheat buns or whole wheat pitas
- Plain Greek yogurt

- Tomato
- Lettuce
- Red Onion

1. Preheat the air fryer to 380°F (193°C).
2. In a food processor, pulse the lentils and parsley mostly smooth. (You will want some bits of lentils in the mixture.)
3. Pour the lentils into a large bowl, and combine with the carrots, onion, bell pepper, jalapeño, garlic, egg, lemon juice, and 1 tablespoon olive oil.
4. Add the onion powder, paprika, oregano, salt, pepper, and bread crumbs. Stir everything together until the seasonings and bread crumbs are well distributed.
5. Form the dough into 4 patties. Place them into the air fryer basket in a single layer, making sure that they don't touch each other. Brush the remaining 1 tablespoon of olive oil over the patties.
6. Bake for 5 minutes. Flip the patties over and bake for an additional 5 minutes.
7. Serve on toasted whole wheat buns or whole wheat pitas with a spoonful of yogurt and lettuce, tomato, and red onion as desired.

CHAPTER 6

FISH AND SEAFOOD

Salmon with Balsamic Maple Glaze

Prep time: 5 minutes | Cook time: 10 minutes | Serves 4

- 4 (6-ounce / 170-g) fillets of salmon
- Salt and freshly ground black pepper
- Olive oil
- ¼ cup pure maple syrup
- 3 tablespoons balsamic vinegar
- 1 teaspoon Dijon mustard

1. Preheat the air fryer to 400ºF (204ºC).
2. Season the salmon well with salt and freshly ground black pepper. Spray or brush the bottom of the air fryer basket with vegetable oil and place the salmon fillets inside. Air fry the salmon for 5 minutes.
3. While the salmon is air frying, combine the maple syrup, balsamic vinegar and Dijon mustard in a small saucepan over medium heat and stir to blend well. Let the mixture simmer while the fish is cooking. It should start to thicken slightly, but keep your eye on it so it doesn't burn.
4. Brush the glaze on the salmon fillets and air fry for an additional 5 minutes. The salmon should feel firm to the touch when finished and the glaze should be nicely browned on top. Brush a little more glaze on top before removing and serving with rice and vegetables, or a nice green salad.

Crab Cake Sliders

Prep time: 5 minutes | Cook time: 10 minutes | Serves 4

- 1 pound (454 g) crab meat, shredded
- ¼ cup whole wheat bread crumbs
- 2 teaspoons dried parsley
- 1 teaspoon salt
- ½ teaspoon freshly ground black
- pepper
- 1 large egg
- 1 teaspoon dry mustard
- 4 whole wheat slider buns
- Sliced tomato, lettuce leaves, and rémoulade sauce, for topping

1. Spray the air fryer basket with olive oil or spray an air fryer–size baking sheet with olive oil or cooking spray.
2. In a medium mixing bowl, combine the crab meat, bread crumbs, parsley, salt, pepper, egg, and dry mustard. Mix well.
3. Form the crab mixture into 4 equal patties. (If your patties are too wet, add an additional 1 to 2 tablespoons of bread crumbs.)
4. Place the crab cakes directly into the greased air fryer basket, or on the greased baking sheet set into the air fryer basket.
5. Set the temperature to 400ºF (204ºC). Set the timer and fry for 5 minutes.
6. Flip the crab cakes. Reset the timer and fry the crab cakes for 5 minutes more.
7. Serve on slider buns with sliced tomato, lettuce, and rémoulade sauce.

Ginger Shrimp Curry with Cilantro

Prep time: 15 minutes | Cook time: 10 minutes | Serves 4

- ¾ cup unsweetened coconut milk
- ¼ cup finely chopped yellow onion
- 2 teaspoons Garam Masala
- 1 tablespoon minced fresh ginger
- 1 tablespoon minced garlic
- 1 teaspoon ground turmeric
- 1 teaspoon salt
- ¼ to ½ teaspoon cayenne pepper
- 1 pound (454 g) raw shrimp (21 to 25 count), peeled and deveined
- 2 teaspoons chopped fresh cilantro

1. In a large bowl, stir together the coconut milk, onion, garam masala, ginger, garlic, turmeric, salt and cayenne, until well blended.
2. Add the shrimp and toss until coated with sauce on all sides. Marinate at room temperature for 30 minutes.
3. Transfer the shrimp and marinade to a 7-inch round baking pan with 4-inch sides. Place the pan in the air fryer basket. Set the air fryer to 375ºF (191ºC) for 10 minutes, stirring halfway through the cooking time.
4. Transfer the shrimp to a serving bowl or platter. Sprinkle with the cilantro and serve.

Lemon Salmon with Parsley

Prep time: 5 minutes | Cook time: 10 minutes | Serves 4

- 3 tablespoons cashew butter
- 1 garlic clove, minced, or ½ teaspoon garlic powder
- 1 teaspoon salt
- 2 tablespoons freshly squeezed lemon juice
- 1 tablespoon minced fresh parsley
- 1 teaspoon minced fresh dill
- 1 teaspoon salt
- ½ teaspoon freshly ground black pepper
- 4 (4-ounce / 113-g) salmon fillets

1. Line the air fryer basket with parchment paper.
2. In a small microwave-safe mixing bowl, combine the cashew butter, garlic, salt, lemon juice, parsley, dill, salt, and pepper.
3. Place the bowl in the microwave and cook on low for about 45 seconds.
4. Meanwhile, place the salmon fillets in the parchment-lined air fryer basket.
5. Spoon the sauce over the salmon.
6. Set the temperature to 400ºF (204ºC). Set the timer and bake for 10 minutes. Since you don't want to overcook the salmon, begin checking for doneness at about 8 minutes. Salmon is done when the flesh is opaque and flakes easily when tested with a fork.

Air Fried Crusted Cod with Lemon

Prep time: 5 minutes | Cook time: 8 to 10 minutes | Serves 2

- 4 tablespoons cashew butter
- 8 to 10 RITZ crackers, crushed into crumbs
- 2 (6-ounce / 170-g) cod fillets
- Salt and freshly ground black pepper
- 1 lemon

1. Preheat the air fryer to 380ºF (193ºC).
2. Heat the butter in a small saucepan on the stovetop or in a microwavable dish in the microwave, and then transfer the butter to a shallow dish. Place the crushed RITZ® crackers into a second shallow dish.
3. Season the fish fillets with salt and freshly ground black pepper. Dip them into the butter and then coat both sides with the RITZ crackers.
4. Place the fish into the air fryer basket and air fry at 380ºF (193ºC) for 8 to 10 minutes, flipping the fish over halfway through the cooking time.
5. Serve with a wedge of lemon to squeeze over the top.

Lemon Garlic Lobster Tails

Prep time: 10 minutes | Cook time: 10 minutes | Serves 2

- 4 ounces (113 g) cashew butter
- 1 tablespoon finely chopped lemon zest
- 1 clove garlic, thinly sliced
- 2 (6-ounce / 170-g) lobster tails
- Salt and freshly ground black pepper
- ½ cup white wine
- ½ lemon, sliced
- Olive oil

1. Start by making the lemon garlic butter. Combine the cashew butter, lemon zest and garlic in a small saucepan. Heat and simmer the butter on the stovetop over the lowest possible heat while you prepare the lobster tails.
2. Prepare the lobster tails by cutting down the middle of the top of the shell. Crack the bottom shell by squeezing the sides of the lobster together so that you can access the lobster meat inside. Pull the lobster tail up out of the shell, but leave it attached at the base of the tail. Lay the lobster meat on top of the shell and season with salt and freshly ground black pepper. Pour a little of the lemon garlic butter on top of the lobster meat and transfer the lobster to the refrigerator so that the butter solidifies a little.
3. Pour the white wine into the air fryer drawer and add the lemon slices. Preheat the air fryer to 400ºF (204ºC) for 5 minutes.
4. Transfer the lobster tails to the air fryer basket. Air fry at 370º for 5 minutes, brushing more butter on halfway through cooking. Remove and serve with more butter for dipping or drizzling.

Shrimp Scampi in White Wine

Prep time: 20 minutes | Cook time: 5 minutes | Serves 2 to 4

- 16 to 20 raw large shrimp, peeled, deveined and tails removed
- ½ cup white wine
- Freshly ground black pepper
- ¼ cup plus 1 tablespoon cashew butter, divided

- 1 clove garlic, sliced
- 1 teaspoon olive oil
- Salt, to taste
- Juice of ½ lemon
- ¼ cup chopped fresh parsley

1. Start by marinating the shrimp in the white wine and freshly ground black pepper for at least 30 minutes, or as long as 2 hours in the refrigerator.
2. Preheat the air fryer to 400ºF (204ºC).
3. Heat ¼ cup of cashew butter in a small saucepan on the stovetop. Add the garlic and let the butter simmer, but be sure to not let it burn.
4. Pour the shrimp and marinade into the air fryer, letting the marinade drain through to the bottom drawer. Drizzle the olive oil on the shrimp and season well with salt. Air fry at 400ºF (204ºC) for 3 minutes. Turn the shrimp over (don't shake the basket because the marinade will splash around) and pour the garlic butter over the shrimp. Air fry for another 2 minutes.
5. Remove the shrimp from the air fryer basket and transfer them to a bowl. Squeeze lemon juice over all the shrimp and toss with the chopped parsley and remaining tablespoon of butter. Season to taste with salt and serve over rice or pasta, or on their own with some crusty bread.

Tuna and Green Beans with Soy Sauce

Prep time: 15 minutes | Cook time: 7 to 12 minutes | Serves 4

- 1 tablespoon olive oil
- 1 red bell pepper, chopped
- 1 cup green beans, cut into 2-inch pieces
- 1 onion, sliced

- 2 cloves garlic, sliced
- 2 tablespoons low-sodium soy sauce
- 1 tablespoon honey
- ½ pound (227 g) fresh tuna, cubed

1. In a 6-inch metal bowl, combine the olive oil, pepper, green beans, onion, and garlic.
2. Cook in the air fryer at 380ºF (193ºC) for 4 to 6 minutes, stirring once, until crisp and tender. Add soy sauce, honey, and tuna, and stir.
3. Cook for another 3 to 6 minutes, stirring once, until the tuna is cooked as desired. Tuna can be served rare or medium-rare, or you can cook it until well done.

Classic Fish and Chips

Prep time: 10 minutes | Cook time: 20 minutes | Serves 4

- 4 (4-ounce / 113-g) fish fillets
- Pinch salt
- Freshly ground black pepper
- ½ teaspoon dried thyme
- 1 egg white
- ¾ cup crushed potato chips
- 2 tablespoons olive oil, divided
- 2 russet potatoes, peeled and cut into strips

1. Pat the fish fillets dry and sprinkle with salt, pepper, and thyme. Set aside.
2. In a shallow bowl, beat the egg white until foamy. In another bowl, combine the potato chips and 1 tablespoon of olive oil and mix until combined.
3. Dip the fish fillets into the egg white, then into the crushed potato chip mixture to coat.
4. Toss the fresh potato strips with the remaining 1 tablespoon olive oil.
5. Use your separator to divide the air fryer basket in half, then air fry the chips and fish at 400ºF (204ºC). The chips will take about 20 minutes; the fish will take about 10 to 12 minutes to cook.

Lime-Cilantro Fried Shrimp

Prep time: 10 minutes | Cook time: 10 minutes | Serves 4

- 1 pound (454 g) raw shrimp, peeled and deveined, with tails on or off
- ½ cup chopped fresh cilantro
- Juice of 1 lime
- 1 egg
- ½ cup whole wheat flour
- ¾ cup whole wheat bread crumbs
- Salt
- Pepper
- Cooking oil
- ½ cup cocktail sauce (optional)

1. Place the shrimp in a plastic bag and add the cilantro and lime juice. Seal the bag. Shake to combine. Marinate in the refrigerator for 30 minutes.
2. In a small bowl, beat the egg. In another small bowl, place the flour. Place the bread crumbs in a third small bowl, and season with salt and pepper to taste.
3. Spray the air fryer basket with cooking oil.
4. Remove the shrimp from the plastic bag. Dip each in the flour, then the egg, and then the bread crumbs.
5. Place the shrimp in the air fryer. It is okay to stack them. Spray the shrimp with cooking oil. Cook at 400ºF (204ºC) for 4 minutes.
6. Open the air fryer and flip the shrimp. I recommend flipping individually instead of shaking to keep the breading intact. Cook for an additional 4 minutes, or until crisp.
7. Cool before serving. Serve with cocktail sauce if desired.

Red Snapper with Orange Salsa

Prep time: 15 minutes | Cook time: 8 minutes | Serves 2

- 2 oranges, peeled, segmented and chopped
- 1 tablespoon minced shallot
- 1 to 3 teaspoons minced red Jalapeño or Serrano pepper
- 1 tablespoon chopped fresh cilantro
- Lime juice, to taste
- Salt, to taste
- 2 (5- to 6-ounce / 142- to 170-g) red snapper fillets
- ½ teaspoon Chinese five spice powder
- Salt and freshly ground black pepper
- Olive oil, in a spray bottle
- 4 green onions, cut into 2-inch lengths

1. Start by making the salsa. Cut the peel off the oranges, slicing around the oranges to expose the flesh. Segment the oranges by cutting in between the membranes of the orange. Chop the segments roughly and combine in a bowl with the shallot, Jalapeño or Serrano pepper, cilantro, lime juice and salt. Set the salsa aside.
2. Preheat the air fryer to 400ºF (204ºC).
3. Season the fish fillets with the five-spice powder, salt and freshly ground black pepper. Spray both sides of the fish fillets with oil. Toss the green onions with a little oil.
4. Transfer the fish to the air fryer basket and scatter the green onions around the fish. Air fry at 400ºF (204ºC) for 8 minutes.
5. Remove the fish from the air fryer, along with the fried green onions. Serve with white rice and a spoonful of the salsa on top.

Italian Tilapia with Lemon Pepper

Prep time: 5 minutes | Cook time: 10 to 11 minutes | Serves 3

- 2 teaspoons Italian seasoning
- 2 teaspoons lemon pepper
- $^1/_3$ cup whole wheat bread crumbs
- $^1/_3$ cup egg whites
- $^1/_3$ cup almond flour
- 3 tilapia fillets
- Olive oil

1. Place the bread crumbs, egg whites, and flour into separate bowls. Mix lemon pepper and Italian seasoning in with bread crumbs.
2. Pat tilapia fillets dry. Dredge in flour, then egg, then bread crumb mixture. Add to air fryer basket and spray lightly with olive oil.
3. Cook 10-11 minutes at 400ºF (204ºC), making sure to flip halfway through cooking.

Lemon Shrimp Caesar Salad

Prep time: 15 minutes | Cook time: 10 minutes | Serves

- 1 large lemon
- 1 pound (454 g) shelled, deveined, large (20 to 24 count) shrimp
- 1 tablespoon olive oil
- 3 garlic cloves, crushed with press
- 1 teaspoon hot paprika
- ⅜ teaspoon salt
- Oil in mister
- 1 head romaine lettuce
- 1 head radicchio
- ¼ cup plain Greek yogurt
- 3 tablespoons finely grated Parmesan cheese
- 1 teaspoon Dijon mustard
- ¼ teaspoon pepper
- 1 cup prepared unseasoned croutons

1. From lemon, grate 1 teaspoon zest and squeeze 3 tablespoons juice. In a large bowl, toss shrimp, olive oil, 2 crushed garlic cloves, hot paprika, lemon zest, and ⅛ teaspoon salt.
2. Preheat air fryer to 390ºF (199ºC). Spray basket with oil. Air fry shrimp in 2 batches, in single layers, 3 minutes per batch, or until cooked.
3. Meanwhile, thinly slice romaine lettuce and radicchio, and place the greens in a large serving bowl. In a small bowl, whisk Greek yogurt, Parmesan cheese, mustard, 1 crushed garlic clove, lemon juice, and ¼ teaspoon each salt and pepper. Toss with lettuce mixture in bowl.
4. Top with shrimp and croutons.

Old Bay Salmon Patties

Prep time: 5 minutes | Cook time: 10 minutes | Serves 4

- 1 (14¾-ounce / 418-g) can wild salmon, drained
- 1 large egg
- ¼ cup diced onion
- ½ cup whole wheat bread crumbs
- 1 teaspoon dried dill
- ½ teaspoon freshly ground black pepper
- 1 teaspoon salt
- 1 teaspoon Old Bay seasoning

1. Spray the air fryer basket with olive oil.
2. Put the salmon in a medium bowl and remove any bones or skin.
3. Add the egg, onion, bread crumbs, dill, pepper, salt, and Old Bay seasoning and mix well.
4. Form the salmon mixture into 4 equal patties.
5. Place the patties in the greased air fryer basket.
6. Set the temperature to 370ºF (188ºC). Set the timer and grill for 5 minutes.
7. Flip the patties. Reset the timer and grill the patties for 5 minutes more.
8. Plate, serve, and enjoy!

Tangy Tilapia with Ginger

Prep time: 10 minutes | Cook time: 8 minutes | Serves 4

- 2 tablespoons olive oil
- 2 tablespoons fresh lime or lemon juice
- 1 teaspoon minced fresh ginger
- 1 clove garlic, minced
- 1 teaspoon ground turmeric
- ½ teaspoon kosher salt
- ¼ to ½ teaspoon cayenne pepper
- 1 pound (454 g) tilapia fillets (2 to 3 fillets)
- Olive oil spray
- Lime or lemon wedges (optional)

1. In a large bowl, combine the oil, lime juice, ginger, garlic, turmeric, salt, and cayenne. Stir until well combined; set aside.
2. Cut each tilapia fillet into three or four equal-size pieces. Add the fish to the bowl and gently mix until all of the fish is coated in the marinade. Marinate for 10 to 15 minutes at room temperature.
3. Spray the air fryer basket with olive oil spray. Place the fish in the basket and spray the fish.
4. Set the air fryer to 325ºF (163ºC) for 3 minutes to partially cook the fish.
5. Set the air fryer to 400ºF (204ºC) for 5 minutes to finish cooking and crisp up the fish.
6. Carefully remove the fish from the basket. Serve hot, with lemon wedges if desired.

Snapper Scampi with Lemon and Garlic

Prep time: 5 minutes | Cook time: 8 to 10 minutes | Serves 4

- 4 (6-ounce / 170-g) skinless snapper or arctic char fillets
- 1 tablespoon olive oil
- 3 tablespoons lemon juice, divided
- ½ teaspoon dried basil
- Pinch salt
- Freshly ground black pepper
- 2 tablespoons cashew butter
- 2 cloves garlic, minced

1. Rub the fish fillets with olive oil and 1 tablespoon of the lemon juice. Sprinkle with the basil, salt, and pepper, and place in the air fryer basket.
2. Grill the fish at 380ºF (193ºC) for 7 to 8 minutes or until the fish just flakes when tested with a fork. Remove the fish from the basket and put on a serving plate. Cover to keep warm.
3. In a 6-by-6-by-2-inch pan, combine the cashew butter, remaining 2 tablespoons lemon juice, and garlic. Cook in the air fryer for 1 to 2 minutes or until the garlic is sizzling. Pour this mixture over the fish and serve.

Dijon Crab-Stuffed Salmon

Prep time: 10 minutes | Cook time: 20 minutes | Serves 4 to 6

- 1 (1½-pound / 680-g) salmon fillet
- Salt and freshly ground black pepper
- 6 ounces (170 g) crab meat
- 1 teaspoon finely chopped lemon zest
- 1 teaspoon Dijon mustard
- 1 tablespoon chopped fresh parsley, plus more for garnish
- 1 scallion, chopped
- ¼ teaspoon salt
- Olive oil

1. Prepare the salmon fillet by butterflying it. Slice into the thickest side of the salmon, parallel to the countertop and along the length of the fillet. Don't slice all the way through to the other side–stop about an inch from the edge. Open the salmon up like a book. Season the salmon with salt and freshly ground black pepper.
2. Make the crab filling by combining the crab meat, lemon zest, mustard, parsley, scallion, salt and freshly ground black pepper in a bowl. Spread this filling in the center of the salmon. Fold one side of the salmon over the filling. Then fold the other side over on top.
3. Transfer the rolled salmon to the center of a piece of parchment paper that is roughly 6- to 7-inches wide and about 12-inches long. The parchment paper will act as a sling, making it easier to put the salmon into the air fryer. Preheat the air fryer to 370ºF (188ºC). Use the parchment paper to transfer the salmon roast to the air fryer basket and tuck the ends of the paper down beside the salmon. Drizzle a little olive oil on top and season with salt and pepper.
4. Air fry the salmon at 370ºF (188ºC) for 20 minutes.
5. Remove the roast from the air fryer and let it rest for a few minutes. Then, slice it, sprinkle some more lemon zest and parsley (or fresh chives) on top and serve.

Coconut Shrimp with Pineapple

Prep time: 15 minutes | Cook time: 5 to 7 minutes | Serves 4

- 1 (8-ounce / 227-g) can crushed pineapple
- ½ cup plain Greek yogurt
- ¼ cup pineapple preserves
- 2 egg whites
- ⅔ cup cornstarch
- ⅔ cup unsweetened coconut
- 1 cup whole wheat bread crumbs
- 1 pound (454 g) uncooked large shrimp, thawed if frozen, deveined and shelled
- Olive oil for misting

1. Drain the crushed pineapple well, reserving the juice.
2. In a small bowl, combine the pineapple, plain Greek yogurt, and preserves, and mix well. Set aside.
3. In a shallow bowl, beat the egg whites with 2 tablespoons of the reserved pineapple liquid. Place the cornstarch on a plate. Combine the coconut and bread crumbs on another plate.
4. Dip the shrimp into the cornstarch, shake it off, then dip into the egg white mixture and finally into the coconut mixture.
5. Place the shrimp in the air fryer basket and mist with oil. Air fry at 400ºF (204ºC) for 5 to 7 minutes or until the shrimp are crisp and golden brown.

Breaded Calamari with Dried Parsley

Prep time: 15 minutes | Cook time: 15 minutes | Serves 4

- Olive oil
- 1 pound (454 g) fresh calamari tubes, rinsed and patted dry
- ½ teaspoon salt, plus more as needed
- ½ teaspoon pepper, plus more as
- needed
- 1 cup whole wheat flour
- 3 eggs
- 1 cup whole wheat bread crumbs
- 2 teaspoons dried parsley

1. Spray a fryer basket lightly with olive oil.
2. Cut the calamari into ¼-inch rings. Season them with salt and black pepper.
3. In a shallow bowl, combine the whole wheat flour and ½ teaspoon of salt and ½ teaspoon of black pepper.
4. In a small bowl, whisk the eggs with 1 teaspoon of water.
5. In another shallow bowl, combine the bread crumbs and parsley.
6. Coat the calamari in the flour mixture, coat in the egg, and dredge in the bread crumbs to coat.
7. Place the calamari in the fryer basket in a single layer. Spray the calamari lightly with olive oil. You may need to cook the calamari in batches.
8. Air fry at 380ºF (193ºC) until crispy and lightly browned, 10 to 15 minutes, shaking the basket a few times during cooking to redistribute and evenly cook.

CHAPTER 7

POULTRY AND MEAT

Buffalo Chicken Drumsticks with Blue Cheese

Prep time: 10 minutes | Cook time: 22 minutes | Serves 2

- 1½ teaspoons paprika
- ½ teaspoon cayenne pepper
- ¼ teaspoon salt
- ¼ teaspoon pepper
- 4 (5-ounce / 142-g) chicken drumsticks, trimmed
- 1 teaspoon vegetable oil
- 3 tablespoons hot sauce
- 2 tablespoons cashew butter
- 2 teaspoons molasses
- ¼ teaspoon cornstarch
- 2 tablespoons crumbled blue cheese

1. Combine paprika, cayenne, salt, and pepper in bowl. Pat drumsticks dry with paper towels. Using metal skewer, poke 10 to 15 holes in skin of each drumstick. Rub with oil and sprinkle evenly with spice mixture.
2. Arrange drumsticks in air fryer basket, spaced evenly apart, alternating ends. Place basket in air fryer and set temperature to 400ºF (204ºC). Cook until chicken is crisp and registers 195ºF (91ºC), 22 to 25 minutes, flipping and rotating chicken halfway through cooking. Transfer chicken to large plate, tent loosely with aluminum foil, and let rest for 5 minutes.
3. Meanwhile, microwave hot sauce, cashew butter, molasses, and cornstarch in large bowl, stirring occasionally, until hot, about 1 minute. Add chicken and toss to coat. Transfer to serving platter and sprinkle with blue cheese. Serve.

Hot Paprika Ribeye

Prep time: 10 minutes | Cook time: 8 minutes | Serves 1 to 2

- ¾ to 1 pound (340 to 454 g) boneless ribeye, at least 1 inch thick
- 1½ teaspoons kosher salt
- 1 teaspoon coconut sugar
- 1 teaspoon coarsely ground black pepper
- ½ teaspoon cumin
- ½ teaspoon coriander
- ¼ teaspoon hot paprika
- Vegetable oil for spraying

1. Pat the steak dry with paper towels. Allow the steak to sit for at least 20 minutes until it is at room temperature. Whisk together the salt, sugar, and spices. Rub both sides of the steak with the spice mixture.
2. Preheat the air fryer to 400ºF (204ºC). Spray the air fryer basket with oil. Place the steak in the air fryer basket. Cook undisturbed at 400ºF (204ºC) for 8 minutes. After 8 minutes, begin checking the internal temperature using a meat thermometer. For medium-rare, cook to 140ºF (60ºC); for medium, 155ºF (68ºC). Continue cooking the steak until you achieve the desired doneness. Allow the meat to rest for 5 minutes before slicing and serving.

Mushroom Meatballs

Prep time: 15 minutes | Cook time: 30 minutes | Serves 4 to 6

- 1 large shallot, finely chopped
- 2 cloves garlic, minced
- 1 tablespoon grated fresh ginger
- 2 teaspoons fresh thyme, finely chopped
- 1½ cups brown mushrooms, very finely chopped
- 2 tablespoons soy sauce
- Freshly ground black pepper
- 1 pound (454 g) ground beef
- ½ pound (227 g) ground pork
- 3 egg yolks
- 1 cup Thai sweet chili sauce (spring roll sauce)
- ¼ cup toasted sesame seeds
- 2 scallions, sliced

1. Combine the shallot, garlic, ginger, thyme, mushrooms, soy sauce, freshly ground black pepper, ground beef and pork, and egg yolks in a bowl and mix the ingredients together. Gently shape the mixture into 24 balls, about the size of a golf ball.
2. Preheat the air fryer to 380ºF (193ºC).
3. Working in batches, air fry the meatballs for 8 minutes, turning the meatballs over halfway through the cooking time. Drizzle some of the Thai sweet chili sauce on top of each meatball and return the basket to the air fryer, air frying for another 2 minutes. Reserve the remaining Thai sweet chili sauce for serving.
4. As soon as the meatballs are done, sprinkle with toasted sesame seeds and transfer them to a serving platter. Scatter the scallions around and serve warm.

Chicken Drumsticks with Peanuts

Prep time: 10 minutes | Cook time: 20 minutes | Serves 4

- 2 tablespoons soy sauce
- ¼ cup rice wine vinegar
- 2 tablespoons chili garlic sauce
- 2 tablespoons sesame oil
- 1 teaspoon minced fresh ginger
- 2 teaspoons honey
- ½ teaspoon ground coriander
- Juice of 1 lime
- 8 chicken drumsticks (about 2½ pounds / 1.1 kg)
- ¼ cup chopped peanuts
- Chopped fresh cilantro
- Lime wedges

1. Combine the soy sauce, rice wine vinegar, chili sauce, sesame oil, ginger, honey, coriander and lime juice in a large bowl and mix together. Add the chicken drumsticks and marinate for 30 minutes.

2. Preheat the air fryer to 370ºF (188ºC).
3. Place the chicken in the air fryer basket. It's ok if the ends of the drumsticks overlap a little. Spoon half of the marinade over the chicken, and reserve the other half.
4. Air fry for 10 minutes. Turn the chicken over and pour the rest of the marinade over the chicken. Air fry for an additional 10 minutes.
5. Transfer the chicken to a plate to rest and cool to an edible temperature. Pour the marinade from the bottom of the air fryer into a small saucepan and bring it to a simmer over medium-high heat. Simmer the liquid for 2 minutes so that it thickens enough to coat the back of a spoon.
6. Transfer the chicken to a serving platter, pour the sauce over the chicken and sprinkle the chopped peanuts on top. Garnish with chopped cilantro and lime wedges.

Chicken, Peppers and Onion Kabobs

Prep time: 10 minutes | Cook time: 45 minutes | Serves 5

- 4 (4-ounce / 113-g) boneless, skinless chicken breasts, cut into 1-inch cubes
- Chicken seasoning or rub
- Salt
- Pepper
- 1 green bell pepper, seeded and cut into 1-inch pieces
- 1 red bell pepper, seeded and cut into 1-inch pieces
- ½ red onion, cut into 1-inch pieces
- Cooking oil

1. Season the chicken with chicken seasoning, salt, and pepper to taste.
2. Thread wooden skewers with the cubed chicken, green bell pepper, red bell pepper, and onion.
3. Spray the air fryer basket with cooking oil.
4. Place the kabobs in the air fryer 4 or 5 at a time, depending on what fits in your unit. Do not overcrowd. You can use an accessory grill pan or rack, or place the kabobs directly into the air fryer basket. Spray the kabobs with cooking oil. Cook at 360ºF (182ºC) for 8 minutes.
5. Open the air fryer and flip the kabobs. Cook for an additional 7 minutes.
6. Remove the cooked kabobs from the air fryer, then repeat steps 4 and 5 for the remaining kabobs.
7. Cool before serving.

Chicken Breasts with Almond Crust

Prep time: 10 minutes | Cook time: 12 minutes | Serves 2

- ½ cup slivered almonds, chopped fine
- ½ cup whole wheat bread crumbs
- 2 tablespoons cashew butter
- 1 teaspoon grated lemon zest, plus lemon wedges for serving
- Salt and pepper
- 1 large egg
- 1 tablespoon whole wheat flour
- 1 teaspoon minced fresh thyme or ½ teaspoon dried
- Pinch cayenne pepper
- 2 (8-ounce / 227-g) boneless, skinless chicken breasts, trimmed

1. Combine almonds, bread crumbs, cashew butter, lemon zest, and ¼ teaspoon salt in bowl and microwave, stirring occasionally, until bread crumbs are light golden brown and almonds are fragrant, about 4 minutes. Transfer to shallow dish and set aside to cool slightly. Whisk egg, flour, thyme, and cayenne together in second shallow dish.
2. Pound chicken to uniform thickness as needed. Pat dry with paper towels and season with salt and pepper. Working with 1 breast at a time, dredge in egg mixture, letting excess drip off, then coat with panko mixture, pressing gently to adhere.
3. Lightly spray base of air fryer basket with vegetable oil spray. Arrange breasts in prepared basket, spaced evenly apart, alternating ends. Place basket in air fryer and set temperature to 400ºF (204ºC). Cook until chicken is crisp and registers 160ºF (71ºC), 12 to 16 minutes, flipping and rotating breasts halfway through cooking. Serve with lemon wedges.

Fennel-Rubbed Pork Tenderloin

Prep time: 15 minutes | Cook time: 16 minutes | Serves 4

- ¼ cup extra-virgin olive oil
- 4 garlic cloves, minced
- 1 tablespoon honey
- 1 teaspoon grated lemon zest plus 2 tablespoons juice
- Salt and pepper
- 2 (1-pound / 454-g) pork tenderloins, trimmed and halved crosswise
- 2 tablespoons fennel seeds, coarsely
- ground
- 4 small zucchini (6 ounces / 170 g each), shaved lengthwise into ribbons
- 2 ounces (57 g) Parmesan cheese, shaved
- 2 tablespoons shredded fresh basil
- 2 tablespoons pine nuts, toasted (optional)

1. Microwave 1 tablespoon oil, garlic, honey, lemon zest, ½ teaspoon salt, and ¼ teaspoon pepper in large bowl until fragrant, about 30 seconds, stirring once halfway through. Pat pork dry with paper towels, add to oil mixture, and toss to coat.
2. Sprinkle pork pieces with fennel seeds, pressing to adhere, then arrange in air fryer basket. (Tuck thinner tail ends of tenderloins under themselves as needed to create uniform pieces.) Place basket in air fryer and set temperature to 350ºF (177ºC). Cook until pork is lightly browned and registers 140ºF (60ºC), 16 to 21 minutes, flipping and rotating tenderloin pieces halfway through cooking. Transfer pork to cutting board, tent with aluminum foil, and let rest while preparing salad.
3. Gently toss zucchini with remaining 3 tablespoons oil, lemon juice, ¼ teaspoon salt, and ¼ teaspoon pepper in clean bowl. Arrange attractively on serving platter and sprinkle with Parmesan, basil, and pine nuts, if using. Slice pork ½ inch thick and serve with salad.

Chicken Thighs with Garlic and Lime

Prep time: 10 minutes | Cook time: 20 minutes | Serves 2

- 3 garlic cloves, minced
- 1 tablespoon grated fresh ginger
- 1½ teaspoons garam masala
- 1 teaspoon ground cumin
- 1 teaspoon chili powder
- 1 teaspoon vegetable oil
- Salt and pepper
- ½ cup plain Greek yogurt
- 4 teaspoons lime juice
- 4 (5-ounce / 142-g) bone-in chicken thighs, trimmed

1. Combine garlic, ginger, garam masala, cumin, chili powder, oil, ¼ teaspoon salt, and ¼ teaspoon pepper in large bowl and microwave until fragrant, about 30 seconds. Set aside to cool slightly, then stir in ¼ cup yogurt and 1 tablespoon lime juice.
2. Pat chicken dry with paper towels. Using metal skewer, poke skin side of chicken 10 to 15 times. Add to bowl with yogurt-spice mixture and toss to coat; set aside to marinate for 10 minutes. Meanwhile, combine remaining ¼ cup yogurt and remaining 1 teaspoon lime juice in clean bowl; season with salt and pepper to taste and set aside.
3. Remove chicken from marinade, letting excess drip off, and arrange skin side up in air fryer basket, spaced evenly apart. Place basket in air fryer and set temperature to 400ºF (204ºC). Cook until chicken is well browned and crisp and registers 195ºF (91ºC), 20 to 30 minutes, rotating chicken halfway through cooking (do not flip).
4. Transfer chicken to serving platter, tent loosely with aluminum foil, and let rest for 5 minutes. Serve with reserved yogurt-lime sauce.

Cheddar Beef Cheeseburgers

Prep time: 5 minutes | Cook time: 20 minutes | Serves 2

- ¾ pound (340 g) lean ground beef
- 3 tablespoons minced onion
- 4 teaspoons ketchup
- 2 teaspoons yellow mustard
- Salt and freshly ground black pepper
- 4 slices of Cheddar cheese, broken into smaller pieces
- 8 hamburger dill pickle chips

1. Combine the ground beef, minced onion, ketchup, mustard, salt and pepper in a large bowl. Mix well to thoroughly combine the ingredients. Divide the meat into four equal portions.
2. To make the stuffed burgers, flatten each portion of meat into a thin patty. Place 4 pickle chips and half of the cheese onto the center of two of the patties, leaving a rim around the edge of the patty exposed. Place the remaining two patties on top of the first and press the meat together firmly, sealing the edges tightly. With the burgers on a flat surface, press the sides of the burger with the palm of your hand to create a straight edge. This will help keep the stuffing inside the burger while it cooks.
3. Preheat the air fryer to 370ºF (188ºC).
4. Place the burgers inside the air fryer basket and air fry for 20 minutes, flipping the burgers over halfway through the cooking time.
5. Serve the cheeseburgers on buns with lettuce and tomato.

Parmesan Turkey Cutlets with Arugula Salad

Prep time: 15 minutes | Cook time: 8 minutes | Serves 4

- 4 turkey breast cutlets (18 ounces / 510 g total)
- Kosher salt and freshly ground black pepper
- 1 large egg, beaten
- ½ cup whole wheat bread crumbs
- 2 tablespoons grated Parmesan
- cheese
- Olive oil spray
- 6 cups baby arugula
- 1 tablespoon olive oil
- 1 tablespoon fresh lemon juice, plus 1 lemon cut into wedges for serving
- Shaved Parmesan (optional)

1. One at a time, place a cutlet between two sheets of parchment paper or plastic wrap. Use a meat mallet or heavy skillet to pound to a ¼-inch thickness. Season the cutlets with ½ teaspoon salt (total) and pepper to taste.
2. Place the egg in a shallow medium bowl. In a separate bowl, combine the bread crumbs and Parmesan. Dip the turkey cutlets in the egg, then in the bread crumb mixture, gently pressing to adhere. Shake off the excess bread crumbs and place on a work surface. Spray both sides with oil.

3. Preheat the air fryer to 400°F (204°C).
4. Working in batches, place the turkey cutlets in the air fryer basket. Cook for about 8 minutes, flipping halfway, until golden brown and the center is cooked. (For a toaster oven–style air fryer, the temperature and timing remain the same.)
5. Place the arugula in a bowl and toss with the oil, lemon juice, ¼ teaspoon salt, and pepper to taste.
6. To serve, place a cutlet on each plate and top with 1½ cups arugula salad. Serve with lemon wedges, and top with some shaved Parmesan, if desired.

Chicken with Sweet Chili Spice

Prep time: 10 minutes | Cook time: 43 minutes | Serves 4

- 1 tablespoon vegetable oil
- 1 (3½-pound / 1.5-kg) chicken, cut into 8 pieces
- Spice Rub:
- 2 tablespoons coconut sugar
- 2 tablespoons paprika
- 1 teaspoon dry mustard powder
- 1 teaspoon chili powder
- 2 tablespoons coarse sea salt or kosher salt
- 2 teaspoons coarsely ground black pepper

1. Prepare the spice rub by combining the coconut sugar, paprika, mustard powder, chili powder, salt and pepper. Rub the oil all over the chicken pieces and then rub the spice mix onto the chicken, covering completely. This is done very easily in a zipper sealable bag. You can do this ahead of time and let the chicken marinate in the refrigerator, or just proceed with cooking right away.
2. Preheat the air fryer to 370°F (188°C).
3. Air fry the chicken in two batches. Place the two chicken thighs and two drumsticks into the air fryer basket. Air fry at 370°F (188°C) for 10 minutes. Then, gently turn the chicken pieces over and air fry for another 10 minutes. Remove the chicken pieces and let them rest on a plate while you cook the chicken breasts. Air fry the chicken breasts, skin side down for 8 minutes. Turn the chicken breasts over and air fry for another 12 minutes.
4. Lower the temperature of the air fryer to 340°F (171°C). Place the first batch of chicken on top of the second batch already in the basket and air fry for a final 3 minutes.
5. Let the chicken rest for 5 minutes and serve warm with some mashed potatoes and a green salad or vegetables.

Pork Tenderloin and Potatoes with Cumin

Prep time: 15 minutes | Cook time: 28 to 30 minutes | Serves 4 to 6

- 3 tablespoons ground cumin
- 1 teaspoon chili powder
- 1 teaspoon kosher salt
- ¼ teaspoon black pepper
- 2 cloves garlic, minced
- 1 pound (454 g) pork tenderloin, cut
- into 2 pieces
- Vegetable oil for spraying
- 1 pound (454 g) Yukon gold potatoes, quartered
- 1 tablespoon extra-virgin olive oil

1. Combine the spices and garlic in a small bowl. Transfer 1 tablespoon of the spice mixture to another bowl and set it aside to season the potatoes. Rub both pieces of the tenderloin with the remaining seasoning mixture. Set aside.
2. Preheat the air fryer to 350ºF (177ºC). Spray the air fryer basket with oil. Place both pieces of tenderloin in the air fryer basket and spray lightly with oil. Cook the tenderloin for approximately 20 minutes, turning halfway through, until a thermometer inserted in the center of the tenderloin reads 145ºF (63ºC). While the tenderloin cooks, place the potatoes in a medium bowl. Add the reserved tablespoon of seasoning mixture and the olive oil. Toss gently to coat the potatoes.
3. Transfer the tenderloin pieces to a platter and tent with foil to rest for 10 minutes. While the tenderloin rests, place the potatoes in the air fryer. Increase the air fryer temperature to 400ºF (204ºC) and cook the potatoes for 8 to 10 minutes, tossing once halfway through cooking, until golden brown. Serve immediately alongside the pork tenderloin.

Chicken Tenders in Dill Pickle Juice

Prep time: 10 minutes | Cook time: 10 to 12 minutes | Serves 4

- 12 chicken tenders (1¼ pounds / 567 g total)
- 1¼ cups dill pickle juice, plus more if needed
- 1 large egg
- 1 large egg white
- ½ teaspoon kosher salt
- Freshly ground black pepper
- 1 cup whole wheat bread crumbs
- Olive oil spray

1. Place the chicken in a shallow bowl and cover with the pickle juice (enough to cover completely). Cover and marinate for 8 hours in the refrigerator.
2. Drain the chicken and pat completely dry with paper towels (discard the marinade).
3. In a medium bowl, beat together the whole egg, egg white, salt, and pepper to taste. In a shallow bowl, place the bread crumbs.

4. Working with one piece at a time, dip the chicken in the egg mixture, then into the bread crumbs, gently pressing to adhere. Shake off any excess bread crumbs and place on a work surface. Generously spray both sides of the chicken with oil.
5. Preheat the air fryer to 400ºF (204ºC).
6. Working in batches, arrange a single layer of the chicken in the air fryer basket. Cook for 10 to 12 minutes, flipping halfway, until cooked through, crispy, and golden. (For a toaster oven–style air fryer, the temperature remains the same; cook for about 10 minutes.) Serve immediately.

Cumin Chicken Breasts with Avocado Salsa

Prep time: 15 minutes | Cook time: 10 minutes | Serves 4

Chicken:
- Kosher salt
- 4 (6-ounce / 170-g) boneless, skinless chicken breasts
- ¾ teaspoon garlic powder
- ½ teaspoon onion powder
- ½ teaspoon ground cumin
- ½ teaspoon ancho chile powder
- ½ teaspoon sweet paprika
- ½ teaspoon dried oregano
- ⅛ teaspoon crushed red pepper flakes
- Olive oil spray

Avocado Salsa:
- ½ cup finely diced red onion
- 3 tablespoons fresh lime juice
- 10 ounces (284 g) avocado (2 medium Hass), diced
- 1 tablespoon chopped fresh cilantro
- Kosher salt

1. For the chicken: Fill a large bowl with lukewarm water and add ¼ cup salt. Stir to dissolve. Let the water cool to room temperature. Add the chicken to the water and refrigerate for at least 1 hour to brine. Remove the chicken from the water and pat dry with paper towels (discard the brine).
2. In a small bowl, combine ¾ teaspoon salt, the garlic powder, onion powder, cumin, ancho powder, paprika, oregano, and pepper flakes. Spritz the chicken all over with oil, then rub with the spice mix.
3. Preheat the air fryer to 380ºF (193ºC).
4. Working in batches, place the chicken breasts in the air fryer basket. Cook for about 10 minutes, flipping halfway, until browned and cooked through.
5. Meanwhile, for the avocado salsa: In a medium bowl, combine the onion and lime juice. Fold in the avocado and cilantro and season with ¼ teaspoon salt.
6. Serve the chicken topped with the salsa.

Top Sirloin Steak with Roasted Mushrooms

Prep time: 15 minutes | Cook time: 25 minutes | Serves 4

- 1½ pounds (680 g) cremini mushrooms, trimmed and halved if large or left whole if small
- 1 cup frozen pearl onions, thawed
- 1 tablespoon extra-virgin olive oil
- 4 garlic cloves, minced
- 2 teaspoons minced fresh thyme or ½ teaspoon dried
- Salt and pepper
- 1 (1½-pound / 680-g) boneless top sirloin steak, 1½ inches thick, trimmed and halved crosswise
- 2 ounces (57 g) blue cheese, crumbled
- ¼ cup heavy cream
- 1 tablespoon chopped fresh parsley

1. Toss mushrooms and onions with 2 teaspoons oil, garlic, thyme, and ½ teaspoon salt in bowl; transfer to air fryer basket. Place basket in air fryer and set temperature to 400ºF (204ºC). Cook until mushrooms and onions begin to brown, 12 to 15 minutes, stirring halfway through cooking.
2. Pat steaks dry with paper towels, rub with remaining 1 teaspoon oil, and season with salt and pepper. Stir mushrooms and onions, then arrange steaks on top, spaced evenly apart. Return basket to air fryer and cook until steaks register 120 to 125ºF (49 to 52ºC) (for medium-rare) or 130 to 135ºF (54 to 57ºC) (for medium), 13 to 18 minutes, flipping and rotating steaks halfway through cooking. Transfer steaks to cutting board and mushroom-onion mixture to serving bowl. Tent each with aluminum foil and let rest while preparing sauce.
3. Microwave ¼ cup blue cheese and cream in bowl, whisking occasionally, until blue cheese is melted and smooth, about 30 seconds, stirring once halfway through. Let sauce cool slightly, then stir in remaining ¼ cup blue cheese. Stir parsley into mushroom-onion mixture and season with salt and pepper to taste. Slice steaks and serve with mushroom-onion mixture and sauce.

Lemon Chicken Wings

Prep time: 10 minutes | Cook time: 20 minutes | Serves 4

- 8 whole chicken wings
- Juice of ½ lemon
- ½ teaspoon garlic powder
- 1 teaspoon onion powder
- Salt
- Pepper
- ¼ cup unsweetened coconut milk
- ½ cup whole wheat flour
- Cooking oil

1. Place the wings in a sealable plastic bag. Drizzle the wings with the lemon juice. Season the wings with the garlic powder, onion powder, and salt and pepper to taste.
2. Seal the bag. Shake thoroughly to combine the seasonings and coat the wings.
3. Pour the coconut milk and the flour into separate bowls large enough to dip the wings.
4. Spray the air fryer basket with cooking oil.
5. One at a time, dip the wings in the coconut milk and then the flour.
6. Place the wings in the air fryer basket. It is okay to stack them on top of each other. Spray the wings with cooking oil, being sure to spray the bottom layer. Cook at 400ºF (204ºC) for 5 minutes.
7. Remove the basket and shake it to ensure all of the pieces will cook fully.
8. Return the basket to the air fryer and continue to cook the chicken. Repeat shaking every 5 minutes until a total of 20 minutes has passed.
9. Cool before serving.

CHAPTER 8

SNACKS AND SWEETS

Popcorn with Garlic Salt

Prep time: 5 minutes | Cook time: 10 minutes | Serves 2

- 2 tablespoons olive oil
- ¼ cup popcorn kernels
- 1 teaspoon garlic salt

1. Preheat the air fryer to 380ºF (193ºC).
2. Tear a square of aluminum foil the size of the bottom of the air fryer and place into the air fryer.
3. Drizzle olive oil over the top of the foil, and then pour in the popcorn kernels.
4. Roast for 8 to 10 minutes, or until the popcorn stops popping.
5. Transfer the popcorn to a large bowl and sprinkle with garlic salt before serving.

Smoked Paprika Cashews

Prep time: 5 minutes | Cook time: 10 minutes | Serves 4

- 2 cups raw cashews
- 2 tablespoons olive oil
- ¼ teaspoon salt
- ¼ teaspoon chili powder
- ⅛ teaspoon garlic powder
- ⅛ teaspoon smoked paprika

1. Preheat the air fryer to 360ºF (182ºC).
2. In a large bowl, toss all of the ingredients together.
3. Pour the cashews into the air fryer basket and roast them for 5 minutes. Shake the basket, then cook for 5 minutes more.
4. Serve immediately.

Sweet Potato Chips

Prep time: 5 minutes | Cook time: 15 minutes | Serves 2

- 1 large sweet potato, sliced thin
- ⅛ teaspoon salt
- 2 tablespoons olive oil

1. Preheat the air fryer to 380ºF (193ºC).
2. In a small bowl, toss the sweet potatoes, salt, and olive oil together until the potatoes are well coated.
3. Put the sweet potato slices into the air fryer and spread them out in a single layer.
4. Fry for 10 minutes. Stir, then air fry for 3 to 5 minutes more, or until the chips reach the preferred level of crispiness.

Coconut and Cranberry Granola Bars

Prep time: 5 minutes | Cook time: 15 minutes | Serves 6

- 2 cups certified gluten-free quick oats
- 2 tablespoons sugar-free dark chocolate chunks
- 2 tablespoons unsweetened dried cranberries
- 3 tablespoons unsweetened shredded coconut
- ½ cup raw honey
- 1 teaspoon ground cinnamon
- ⅛ teaspoon salt
- 2 tablespoons olive oil

1. Preheat the air fryer to 360ºF (182ºC). Line an 8-by-8-inch baking dish with parchment paper that comes up the side so you can lift it out after cooking.
2. In a large bowl, mix together all of the ingredients until well combined.
3. Press the oat mixture into the pan in an even layer.
4. Place the pan into the air fryer basket and bake for 15 minutes.
5. Remove the pan from the air fryer and lift the granola cake out of the pan using the edges of the parchment paper.
6. Allow to cool for 5 minutes before slicing into 6 equal bars.
7. Serve immediately, or wrap in plastic wrap and store at room temperature for up to 1 week.

Honey Spiced Nuts

Prep time: 10 minutes | Cook time: 25 minutes | Makes 3 cups

- 1 egg white, lightly beaten
- ¼ cup honey
- 1 teaspoon salt
- ½ teaspoon ground cinnamon
- ¼ teaspoon ground cloves
- ¼ teaspoon ground allspice
- Pinch ground cayenne pepper
- 1 cup pecan halves
- 1 cup cashews
- 1 cup almonds

1. Combine the egg white with the honey and spices in a bowl.
2. Preheat the air fryer to 300ºF (149ºC).
3. Spray or brush the air fryer basket with vegetable oil. Toss the nuts together in the spiced egg white and transfer the nuts to the air fryer basket.
4. Air fry for 25 minutes, stirring the nuts in the basket a few times during the cooking process. Taste the nuts (carefully because they will be very hot) to see if they are crunchy and nicely toasted. Air fry for a few more minutes if necessary.
5. Serve warm or cool to room temperature and store in an airtight container for up to two weeks.

Honey Chocolate Lava Cake

Prep time: 5 minutes | Cook time: 10 minutes | Serves 4

- Olive oil cooking spray
- ¼ cup whole wheat flour
- 1 tablespoon unsweetened dark chocolate cocoa powder
- ⅛ teaspoon salt
- ½ teaspoon baking powder
- ¼ cup honey
- 1 egg
- 2 tablespoons olive oil

1. Preheat the air fryer to 380°F (193°C). Lightly coat the insides of four ramekins with olive oil cooking spray.
2. In a medium bowl, combine the flour, cocoa powder, salt, baking powder, honey, egg, and olive oil.
3. Divide the batter evenly among the ramekins.
4. Place the filled ramekins inside the air fryer and bake for 10 minutes.
5. Remove the lava cakes from the air fryer and slide a knife around the outside edge of each cake. Turn each ramekin upside down on a saucer and serve.

Mini Mixed Berry Pie

Prep time: 10 minutes | Cook time: 15 minutes | Serves 4

- Cooking spray
- ¼ cup honey
- 2 tablespoons cornstarch
- ¼ teaspoon vanilla extract
- ½ teaspoon loosely packed grated orange zest
- 1 cup halved and sliced strawberries
- ⅔ cup raspberries
- ⅔ cup blueberries
- ⅔ cup blackberries, cut into thirds
- 1 store-bought refrigerated piecrust
- 1 large egg

1. Spray a 5½-inch mini pie dish with cooking spray.
2. In a medium bowl, combine the honey, cornstarch, vanilla, and orange zest and mix well. Add the strawberries, raspberries, blueberries, and blackberries and gently toss to combine. Transfer the mixture to the pie dish.
3. Lay the prepared dough on a work surface, then cut out a 7-inch-diameter round. Refrigerate the remaining crust for another recipe. Place the piecrust over the baking dish and crimp the edges to create a seal. Cut 4 slits around the center of the piecrust.
4. In a small bowl, beat the egg with 1 tablespoon water. Using a pastry brush, brush the top of the crust with the egg wash.
5. Preheat the air fryer to 350°F (177°C).
6. Place the pie in the air fryer basket. Bake for about 15 minutes, until the crust is golden and the berries are hot and bubbling. Let cool for at least 15 minutes before cutting so the filling will thicken. Serve warm.

Sweet Paprika Onion Rings

Prep time: 10 minutes | Cook time: 10 minutes | Serves 4

- 1 medium Vidalia onion (about 9 ounces / 255 g)
- 1½ cups cornflakes
- ½ cup whole wheat bread crumbs
- ½ teaspoon sweet paprika
- ½ cup unsweetened coconut milk
- 1 large egg
- ¼ cup whole wheat flour
- ½ teaspoon kosher salt
- Olive oil spray

1. Trim the ends off the onion, then quarter the onion crosswise (about ⅓-inch-thick slices) and separate into rings.
2. In a food processor, pulse the cornflakes until fine. Transfer to a medium bowl and stir in the bread crumbs and paprika. In another medium bowl, whisk together the coconut milk, egg, flour, and ½ teaspoon salt until combined.
3. Working in batches, dip the onion rings in the coconut milk batter, then into the cornflake mixture to coat. Set aside on a work surface and spray both sides with oil.
4. Preheat the air fryer to 340ºF (171ºC).
5. Working in batches, arrange a single layer of the onion rings in the air fryer basket. Cook for about 10 minutes, flipping halfway, until golden brown. Serve immediately.

Russet Potato Fries

Prep time: 10 minutes | Cook time: 30 minutes | Serves 2

- 2 to 3 russet potatoes, peeled and cut into ¼-inch sticks
- 2 to 3 teaspoons olive or vegetable oil
- Salt

1. Cut the potatoes into ¼-inch strips. (A mandolin with a julienne blade is really helpful here.) Rinse the potatoes with cold water several times and let them soak in cold water for at least 10 minutes or as long as overnight.
2. Preheat the air fryer to 380ºF (193ºC).
3. Drain and dry the potato sticks really well, using a clean kitchen towel. Toss the fries with the oil in a bowl and then air fry the fries in two batches at 380ºF (193ºC) for 15 minutes, shaking the basket a couple of times while they cook.
4. Add the first batch of French fries back into the air fryer basket with the finishing batch and let everything warm through for a few minutes. As soon as the fries are done, season them with salt and transfer to a plate or basket. Serve them warm with ketchup or your favorite dip.

Pineapple with Lime and Mint

Prep time: 5 minutes | Cook time: 30 minutes | Serves 4

- 1 pineapple
- 4 tablespoons cashew butter
- 2 tablespoons plus 2 teaspoons coconut sugar
- 2 tablespoons fresh mint, cut into ribbons
- 1 lime

1. Cut off the top and bottom of the pineapple and stand it on a cut end. Slice off the outer skin, cutting deeply enough to remove the eyes of the pineapple. Cut off any pointy edges to make the pineapple nice and round. Cut the peeled pineapple into 8 circles, approximately ½ to ¾ inch (1.3 to 2 cm) thick. Remove the core of each slice using a small, circular cookie or biscuit cutter, or simply cut out the core using a paring knife. Place the pineapple rings on a plate.
2. Brush both sides of the pineapple rings with the cashew butter. Working in 2 batches, arrange 4 slices in a single layer in the basket of the air fryer. Sprinkle ½ teaspoon coconut sugar on the top of each ring. Cook at 400ºF (204ºC) until the top side is browned and caramelized, about 10 minutes. With tongs, carefully flip each ring and sprinkle coconut sugar on the second side. Cook for an additional 5 minutes until the second side is browned and caramelized. Remove the cooked pineapple and repeat with the remaining pineapple rings.
3. Arrange all the cooked pineapple rings on a serving plate or platter. Sprinkle with mint and spritz with the juice of the lime. Serve warm.

Roasted Apples with Walnuts and Honey

Prep time: 5 minutes | Cook time: 12 t0 15 minutes | Serves 4

- 2 Granny Smith apples
- ¼ cup certified gluten-free rolled oats
- 2 tablespoons honey
- ½ teaspoon ground cinnamon
- 2 tablespoons chopped walnuts
- Pinch salt
- 1 tablespoon olive oil

1. Preheat the air fryer to 380ºF (193ºC).
2. Core the apples and slice them in half.
3. In a medium bowl, mix together the oats, honey, cinnamon, walnuts, salt, and olive oil.
4. Scoop a quarter of the oat mixture onto the top of each half apple.
5. Place the apples in the air fryer basket, and roast for 12 to 15 minutes, or until the apples are fork-tender.

Blueberry and Oats Crisp

Prep time: 5 minutes | Cook time: 15 minutes | Serves 8

- 1 cup rolled oats
- ½ cup whole wheat flour
- ¼ cup extra-virgin olive oil
- ¼ teaspoon salt
- 1 teaspoon cinnamon
- $1/_3$ cup honey
- Cooking oil
- 4 cups blueberries (thawed if frozen)

1. In a large bowl, combine the rolled oats, flour, olive oil, salt, cinnamon, and honey.
2. Spray a barrel pan with cooking oil all over the bottom and sides of the pan.
3. Spread the blueberries on the bottom of the barrel pan. Top with the oat mixture.
4. Place the pan in the air fryer. Cook at 350ºF (177ºC) for 15 minutes.
5. Cool before serving.

Green Plantain with Garlic Powder

Prep time: 5 minutes | Cook time: 16 minutes | Serves 2

- 1 large green plantain
- Kosher salt
- ¾ teaspoon garlic powder
- Olive oil spray

1. With a sharp knife, trim the ends of the plantain. To make it easier to peel, score a slit along the length of the plantain skin. Cut the plantain crosswise into eight 1-inch pieces and peel the skin off each piece.
2. In a small bowl, combine 1 cup water with 1 teaspoon salt and the garlic powder.
3. Preheat the air fryer to 400ºF (204ºC).
4. Spritz the plantain all over with olive oil and transfer to the air fryer basket. Cook for 6 minutes, shaking halfway, until soft. Immediately transfer to a work surface. While they are still hot, use a tostonera or the bottom of a glass jar or measuring cup to flatten each piece.
5. Dip each piece, one at a time, in the seasoned water, then transfer to the work surface (discard the water). Generously spray both sides of the plantain with oil.
6. Preheat the air fryer to 400ºF (204ºC) again.
7. Working in batches, arrange a single layer of the plantain in the air fryer basket. Cook for about 10 minutes, flipping halfway, until golden and crisp. Transfer to a serving dish. While still hot, spray lightly with olive oil and season with ⅛ teaspoon salt. Serve immediately.

Cinnamon Donut Holes

Prep time: 5 minutes | Cook time: 20 minutes | Makes 16 donut holes

- 1 (8-ounce / 227-g) can jumbo biscuit dough
- Cooking oil
- 1 tablespoon stevia
- 2 tablespoons cinnamon

1. Form the biscuit dough evenly into 16 balls, 1 to 1½ inches thick.
2. Spray the air fryer basket with cooking oil.
3. Place 8 donut holes in the air fryer. Do not stack. Spray them with cooking oil. Cook at 360ºF (182ºC) for 4 minutes.
4. Open the air fryer and flip the donut holes. Cook for an additional 4 minutes.
5. Remove the cooked donut holes, then repeat steps 3 and 4 for the remaining 8 donut holes. Allow the donut holes to cool.
6. In a small bowl, combine the stevia and cinnamon and stir.
7. Spritz the donut holes with cooking oil. Dip the donut holes in the cinnamon and sugar mixture, and serve.

Peach Ice Cream with Almonds

Prep time: 5 minutes | Cook time: 10 minutes | Serves 4

- 4 peaches, halved and pitted
- 1 cup vanilla ice cream, frozen yogurt, or dairy-free ice cream
- 2 tablespoons slivered almonds
- 4 sprigs spearmint, for garnish

1. Preheat the air fryer to 375ºF (191ºC).
2. Working in batches, arrange a single layer of peach halves cut sides up in the air fryer basket. Cook for about 10 minutes, until the peaches are soft and golden brown on top. (For a toaster oven–style air fryer, the temperature remains the same; cook for about 8 minutes.)
3. Divide the peaches among 4 serving bowls. Place 2-tablespoon scoops of ice cream in the center of each peach half. Top with the slivered almonds and mint and serve immediately.

Cinnamon-Honey Churros

Prep time: 5 minutes | Cook time: 20 to 22 minutes | Serves 5

- ¼ teaspoon kosher salt
- 2 tablespoons cashew butter
- 3 tablespoons honey
- 1 cup whole wheat flour
- 1 teaspoon vanilla extract
- Olive oil spray
- ½ teaspoon ground cinnamon

1. In a medium pot, combine 1 cup water, the salt, 1 tablespoon of the cashew butter, and 1 tablespoon of the honey. Bring to a boil over medium-high heat. Once boiling, remove from the heat and add the flour and vanilla. Mix with a wooden spoon until thoroughly combined and a dough-ball forms. Let cool for 5 minutes.
2. Transfer the dough to a plastic pastry bag fitted with a star tip, pushing the dough into the bottom (see Skinny Scoop). Twist the top of the bag to keep it closed. Pipe 10 (5-inch-long) strips of dough onto a plate or work surface and spray with oil.
3. Preheat the air fryer to 340ºF (171ºC).
4. Working in batches, arrange the churros in a single layer in the air fryer basket. Cook for 20 to 22 minutes, flipping halfway, until golden.
5. Meanwhile, melt the remaining tablespoon cashew butter in a small bowl. On a small plate, combine the remaining 2 tablespoons honey and the cinnamon and mix well.
6. Remove the churros from the air fryer and transfer to a plate or work surface. Use a pastry brush to lightly brush each with cashew butter, then roll in the cinnamon-honey mixture. Repeat with the remaining churros. Serve immediately.

Appendix 1 Measurement Conversion Chart

VOLUME EQUIVALENTS(DRY)

US STANDARD	METRIC (APPROXIMATE)
1/8 teaspoon	0.5 mL
1/4 teaspoon	1 mL
1/2 teaspoon	2 mL
3/4 teaspoon	4 mL
1 teaspoon	5 mL
1 tablespoon	15 mL
1/4 cup	59 mL
1/2 cup	118 mL
3/4 cup	177 mL
1 cup	235 mL
2 cups	475 mL
3 cups	700 mL
4 cups	1 L

WEIGHT EQUIVALENTS

US STANDARD	METRIC (APPROXIMATE)
1 ounce	28 g
2 ounces	57 g
5 ounces	142 g
10 ounces	284 g
15 ounces	425 g
16 ounces (1 pound)	455 g
1.5 pounds	680 g
2 pounds	907 g

VOLUME EQUIVALENTS(LIQUID)

US STANDARD	US STANDARD (OUNCES)	METRIC (APPROXIMATE)
2 tablespoons	1 fl.oz.	30 mL
1/4 cup	2 fl.oz.	60 mL
1/2 cup	4 fl.oz.	120 mL
1 cup	8 fl.oz.	240 mL
1 1/2 cup	12 fl.oz.	355 mL
2 cups or 1 pint	16 fl.oz.	475 mL
4 cups or 1 quart	32 fl.oz.	1 L
1 gallon	128 fl.oz.	4 L

TEMPERATURES EQUIVALENTS

FAHRENHEIT(F)	CELSIUS(C) (APPROXIMATE)
225 °F	107 °C
250 °F	120 °C
275 °F	135 °C
300 °F	150 °C
325 °F	160 °C
350 °F	180 °C
375 °F	190 °C
400 °F	205 °C
425 °F	220 °C
450 °F	235 °C
475 °F	245 °C
500 °F	260 °C

Appendix 2 The Dirty Dozen and Clean Fifteen

The Environmental Working Group (EWG) is a nonprofit, nonpartisan organization dedicated to protecting human health and the environment Its mission is to empower people to live healthier lives in a healthier environment. This organization publishes an annual list of the twelve kinds of produce, in sequence, that have the highest amount of pesticide residue-the Dirty Dozen-as well as a list of the fifteen kinds ofproduce that have the least amount of pesticide residue-the Clean Fifteen.

THE DIRTY DOZEN

- The 2016 Dirty Dozen includes the following produce. These are considered among the year's most important produce to buy organic:

Strawberries	Spinach
Apples	Tomatoes
Nectarines	Bell peppers
Peaches	Cherry tomatoes
Celery	Cucumbers
Grapes	Kale/collard greens
Cherries	Hot peppers

- *The Dirty Dozen list contains two additional itemskale/collard greens and hot peppers-because they tend to contain trace levels of highly hazardous pesticides.*

THE CLEAN FIFTEEN

- The least critical to buy organically are the Clean Fifteen list. The following are on the 2016 list:

Avocados	Papayas
Corn	Kiw
Pineapples	Eggplant
Cabbage	Honeydew
Sweet peas	Grapefruit
Onions	Cantaloupe
Asparagus	Cauliflower
Mangos	

- *Some of the sweet corn sold in the United States are made from genetically engineered (GE) seedstock. Buy organic varieties of these crops to avoid GE produce.*

Appendix 3 Recipe Index